Forever Young

Forever Young

Ten Gifts of Faith for the Graduate

Pat Williams
Karen Kingsbury

Health Communications, Inc.
Deerfield Beach, Florida

www.bcibooks.com

Library of Congress Cataloging-in-Publication Data
is available from the Library of Congress.

Publisher: Faith Communications, Inc.
           An Imprint of Health Communications, Inc.
           3201 S.W. 15th Street
           Deerfield Beach, FL 33442–8190

Cover design by Andrea Perrine Brower
Inside book design by Lawna Patterson Oldfield

Pat's Dedication

This book is dedicated to our first two grandchildren,
Laila Michelle and Brianna Lee.
I pray that the lessons shared between these covers
will impact their lives as well as yours.

Karen's Dedication

To Donald, my prince charming,
Kelsey, my forever laughter,
Tyler, my beautiful song,
Sean, my silly heart,
Josh, my gentle giant,
EJ, my chosen one,
Austin, my miracle boy.

And to God Almighty, who has—for now—
blessed me with these.

Contents

Acknowledgments

With deep appreciation I acknowledge the support and guidance of the following people who helped make this book possible:

Special thanks to Bob Vander Weide and John Weisbrod of the Orlando Magic.

I'm grateful to my assistant, Diana Basch, who managed so many of the details that made this book possible.

Hats off to four dependable associates—Andrew Herdliska, my advisor Ken Hussar, Vince Pileggi of the Orlando Magic mail/copy room, and my ace typist, Fran Thomas.

Hearty thanks are also due to Peter Vegso and his fine staff at Health Communications, Inc., and to my partner in writing this book, Karen Kingsbury. Thank you all for believing that I had something important to share and for providing the support and the forum to say it.

And finally, special thanks and appreciation go to my wife, Ruth, and to my wonderful and supportive family. They are truly the backbone of my life.

Foreword

by Dwight Howard
Nineteen-year-old NBA star of Orlando Magic

Just a few short months ago I was in exactly the same position you are in. I was getting ready to graduate from high school in Atlanta and wondering what opportunities lay ahead for me. I had made a decision not to go to college and instead to try to make it as an NBA player at the age of eighteen. That was a pretty lofty goal, but in late June 2004, the Orlando Magic made me the number one pick in the draft. Needless to say, that was an exciting moment in my life.

When I arrived in Orlando, I had the opportunity to meet Pat Williams, the senior vice president of the Magic. He is a longtime NBA executive and the father of nineteen children, including fourteen adopted from four foreign countries. There was a year when sixteen of Pat's children were all teenagers at the same time!

When Pat speaks to young people, I encourage them to listen because he knows what he's talking about. His new book, *Forever Young,* will impact your life in a powerful way. There is so much wise advice for you to consider.

You'll learn about the importance of having dreams and goals in life. Then you'll learn how hard you must work to reach those goals. Through the tough times of life, you learn that you must persevere to have those dreams come true. I can relate to everything Pat writes about.

One of my favorite chapters is about being a lifelong learner. As a newcomer to the NBA, I'm learning something every time I go out on the floor. I want to be the best player I can be, so I must never stop learning how to get better.

Threaded throughout this book are powerful spiritual truths. Pat Williams is a committed Christian leader. I'm grateful he is. We both agree that the most important decision any person will ever make is the decision to accept Christ as Savior and Lord and then follow him on a daily basis. Pat's new book will show you how to do that.

I'm still a teenager just like you, but even when I'm an old man, I want to be forever young in my mind and spirit. I'm sure you want the same. This book will help you get started.

God bless you always,

Dwight Howard

Orlando Magic

May 2005

Introduction

Congratulations, graduates!

You've reached what is probably the greatest goal of your lives so far, and you're ready for whatever lies ahead, whatever is next on your adult journey. You're excited and enthusiastic, tenderhearted and overjoyed.

But you have some concerns.

You've seen the way many adults are, and you're sure you don't want to be like them. You know the ones I'm talking about. The neighbor with the permanent scowl on his face; the uncle who looks bent and old under the burden of a job he can't stand; your friend's parents who fight constantly and look aged beyond their years.

No way you want to wind up like them, right?

So how do you go through the next twenty, thirty, forty years and maintain the joy you feel today? How do you hold on to enthusiasm and hope and optimism? How can you live your life forever young?

For the past three decades I've been collecting wisdom and anecdotes from people who managed to stay young regardless of their age. Looking over the thousands of pieces of research in my files, I saw common threads, trends among those who were young at heart, those who still knew how to embrace life even into their nineties.

I've taken these common threads and woven them into ten gifts of faith for you:

- God's the Glue
- Dare to Dream
- Live Healthy
- Don't Give Up
- Work Hard and Happy

- Be a Lifelong Learner
- Laugh Long and Loud
- Choose to Dance
- Handle the Hard Times
- Love Easily and Often

Read through the chapters, breathe in the truth from these people, and focus on the type of life you'll need to live if you want to stay young at heart. This is the key to success—not the goals you'll achieve, but the way you approach life along the way.

Success is not a destination; it's a journey. Conrad Hilton, the famous hotelier, said, "Success seems to be connected with action. Successful people keep moving." Author John C. Maxwell said, "Success is not an event. It is an ongoing process we engage in, time and time again."

Life is short, graduates. Squeeze the most out of every day, every moment. You can start by grabbing hold of these ten truths that will help you stay forever young. The fountain of youth may be as close as the next chapter!

Aim high,
Pat Williams

ONE

God's the Glue

If you're going to hold on to the enthusiasm you have for life today, if you're going to hold on to the dreams and delight of today, you'll need to know one thing for sure: God's the glue.

Only a relationship with Jesus Christ will allow you to keep your childlike heart, the joy and hope you carry with you today. If you don't have that assurance of salvation, find it. Take a look at the Bible, read the book of John, connect with a Bible-believing church, and dive into the wonderful world of faith in Christ.

Get this part right, and the next nine principles will be a lot easier.

The following sections tell about adults who are living life still young at heart, adults who know that their faith is the basis for that youthful life.

Give God the Title Deed

The late Dr. Bill Bright, founder of Campus Crusade for Christ, often referred to a decision he and his wife made in the spring of 1951.

It was a decision to become—as Bill liked to say it—slaves to Jesus Christ. Total, absolute, sold-out, surrendered slaves to Christ.

"We wrote and signed over the 'title deeds' of our lives to Him, and a day later God gave the two of us a vision for the Campus Crusade ministry."

The way Bill viewed it, after deciding to live for Jesus Christ, he was no longer his own. Rather he had been bought with a price—the price of Christ's blood shed on the cross. Bill would tell people, "If God can create and rule the universe, think about what He can do for us and through us, if we ask Him to do so."

Every day after that decision, Bill Bright would get down on his knees and give gratitude and praise to Jesus for being his Savior. He would tell the Lord, "Jesus, I want to be close to You. Walk in my body, think with my mind, love with my heart, speak with my lips. Do whatever You want in and through me. Take my attitudes, my motives, my words, my actions, my desires and orchestrate them by Your Holy Spirit."

Forever Young in War

In the warm dawn hours in Iraq that April day in 2003, NBC news correspondent David Bloom grabbed his phone and played back his messages. Halfway through the recording was a long message from Jim Lane, a New York financier. It had become habit for the men to share a daily long-distance devotion using Oswald Chambers' classic book, *My Utmost for His Highest*. Lane read the message for April 5, an inspirational piece taken from Matthew 24. "Because of what the

Son of Man went through, every human being can now get through into the very presence of God."

Bloom—who had been sitting in a modified tank—then climbed out, took a few steps, and collapsed, dead instantly. Less than a minute later, he was experiencing the reality of Matthew 24—finding his way through to the very presence of God.

Bloom's death was a devastating shock to his family and the nation. He was regularly watched by millions of viewers as he traversed across the desert, covering the story of the war in Iraq. At age thirty-nine he was a prime example of living forever young, of realizing that God's the glue if you're determined to hold on to the excitement of youth.

For there was a side to David Bloom, TV correspondent, that the nation did not see. David was a devout believer in Jesus Christ. He grew up in the church, but two years before his death, he truly came to a saving knowledge of Jesus, a knowledge that started his greatest journey of all—his journey into eternal life.

Meeting God Weekly

Bloom joined a weekly men's discipleship group founded by Jim Lane. While attending meetings, he developed friendships with some of the great men of the Christian faith, including Chuck Colson, founder of Prison Fellowship. During that time, it was clear to all who knew him that Bloom had a hunger for God that demanded he continue studying the Bible.

On the day he died, friends say Bloom was in a very good place, at peace with himself, his family and his God. That peace was evident in the last message he sent his wife. There—in the midst of a battlefield—David Bloom's own mortality was evidently on his mind.

Bloom wrote, "When the moment comes, in my life, when you are talking about my last day, I am determined that you and others will say, 'He was devoted to his wife and children; he was admired; he gave every ounce of his being for those whom he cared most about . . . not himself, but God and his family.'"

The lasting image of David Bloom—one that will remain in the memories of his family and the American public—was that of a youthful man, bouncing across the Iraqi desert, poking his head out of an armored tank. His dirt-streaked face and wind-blown hair did nothing to cover the sheer exuberance of his living life to the full, at peace with God and himself—a picture of a life lived forever young.

Jesus, Anyone?

Resolve that you'll live your life in a way that other people will know about your faith. If they spend any significant amount of time with you, they'll see your actions or hear your conversation or become aware of your convictions, and your faith will be as obvious as the rising sun.

It was important to Brian Vahaly, internationally ranked tennis player, that people saw him as a Christian. "I wanted them to see the way I lived and because of that, to trust me!" As the trust grew, Vahaly would have an opportunity to share his faith. How did he do that? Whenever he roomed with a teammate or traveled with one, he saw it as a chance to make a difference in someone's life. Tennis can be a great avenue for telling someone the truth!

The faith-walk that keeps a person young, will also keep a person eager about sharing his faith. Who in your life today needs to hear the good news about Jesus? Be willing to share your faith with your friends.

I Never Thought of That

You've made it through school, you've graduated, and you probably have the next goal in mind. But there are a few things you may not have thought about:

Bill Selby of the St. Louis Cardinals says that the amazing thing about being a Christian and growing closer to the Lord is that the more we mature as Christians, the more we see how far away we are.

"I know God is shaping every inch of my life," Selby has said. "He's allowing me to see where I stand with Him and how thankful I am that He's selected me to be His child."

Likewise, most people don't think about their dream job as anything other than a job or a career. Not NFL quarterback Kurt Warner. He sees his job as a platform.

"God has given me an unbelievable platform that reaches an enormous amount of people," he says.

Warner understands that part of his platform is the pain that has come to his family. His son was injured at a young age and has some physical and mental disabilities. His wife lost her parents in a tornado, and at one point Warner worked as a stock boy at a grocery store.

"We've had difficult times—our son, my wife's parents, us financially —and then we had success," Warner said. "We can touch an unbelievable amount of people and speak to them on a lot of different levels because of that. That's the way I like to look at all we've been through."

Cowboy Up

The Lord wants you to give everything up to him: your career, your energy, your talents. Along the way, there will be stumbles and falls, trip-ups and temptations. They will be fewer if you determine to give your life to Christ and avoid compromising situations.

So many people have lost everything because of an illicit affair, an illegal business deal, or a life riddled with drugs and alcohol. Those people look older than their years, worn and weathered, with worry lines across their foreheads and around their eyes.

A life lived for self and pleasure, a life of careless sin, is a life that ages people quickly. Living life for Christ will ease the lines in your face and make you youthful in every sense.

When I'm on the road, I like to stay in my room and order room service. Sometimes I hang out with other Christian guys. I never go out to go out. I don't enjoy it. I love my wife and I take my marriage very personally and to heart. Whenever you commit to those vows, they're for life.

Tom Landry, longtime coach of the Dallas Cowboys, was known for his strong Christian faith. Landry said, "Faith gives a man hope, and hope is what life is all about. That's why won-lost records, championships and all that has gone on in the past, really have so little meaning for me. All that is nice, of course. But it's not what matters most. . . . I live my life for Christ in every area, and I work hard because God expects us to be the best we can."

Take the advice of a Cowboy.

Privacy Schmivacy

On one occasion, Senator Robert Pittenger and my friend Dr. Bill Bright, founder of Campus Crusade, met with former Texas governor and presidential candidate John Connally. After a long discussion on world affairs, Bill asked the governor if he knew Jesus. The governor, a confident man, pulled himself up an inch or so and said, "Dr. Bright, I don't believe in wearing my religion on my sleeve. It's a personal thing."

Then, in a firm but sensitive tone, Bill said, "Governor, Jesus Christ died for you in a very public way. It wasn't just a private thing to Him." Bill then presented the governor with the Gospel, and left him material on how to know Christ.

Eight months later, the governor spoke at a major Campus Crusade event. The first words out of his mouth were, "Jesus said, 'I am the light of the world. If you follow me, you will not stumble in the darkness.'"

If you believe in Christ, tell someone else. It's no fun staying young and vibrant all by yourself!

Presidential Power

President George W. Bush makes no apology for his faith-based leadership. In their book on the president, Carolyn B. Thompson and James W. Ware include a quote that sheds light on the man's deep, abiding faith.

"I could not have been Governor if I didn't believe in a divine plan that supersedes all human plans. Politics is a fickle business. Polls change. Today's friend is tomorrow's adversary. People lavish praise and attention. Many times it is genuine, and sometimes it is not.

"Yet, I build my life on a foundation that will not shift. My faith frees me. It frees me to put the problems of the moment in proper perspective. It frees me to make decisions that others might not like. It frees me to try to do the right thing, even though it may not poll well."

Bible Biggie

One way to stay young is to walk in perfect faith. I'm not talking about perfect performance, because none of us will be perfect. But if your faith and trust, your belief and hope in Jesus are right, everything else will fall in place.

Read these words that shout at us from the pages of Isaiah 43:2–5 (NASB).

> When you pass through the waters, I will be with you; and through the rivers, they will not overflow you. When you walk through the fire, you will not be scorched, nor will the flame burn you. For I am the Lord, your God, The Holy One of Israel, your Savior; . . . since you are precious in My sight, since you are honored and I love you, . . . do not fear, for I am with you."

God did not say the rushing waters wouldn't come. He did not say we wouldn't see the flames or feel the heat. Instead he said *in* the rising waters, He would be with us. He said *in* the middle of the fire, he would be with us. He provides for us in times of need.

Want some good news? Nothing surprises God, nothing catches him off-guard. He knows exactly what he's going to do in every situation. God is never befuddled by any situation, no matter how hard or desperate it seems to us.

I have a pastor friend in Atlanta, Johnny Hunt, who says, "Did it ever occur to you that nothing ever occurs to God?"

Faith means believing that even when we can't see the way from here to there, God is in control. End of story. Believe it, live like you believe it, and you'll be on your way to capturing a view of what it's like to live forever young.

Rev Up the Race Car

How can you rev up the engines of your spiritual lives? Very simply, you must pray. Prayer is our act of talking to God. When we don't pray, we walk through life with our greatest friend at our side, never talking to him.

Race car driver Scott Sharp once said, "I spend some time in prayer every day of my life; not just when I'm driving race cars. I don't know how other people who aren't Christians, who don't have a relationship with God, can handle all the distractions, pressures and concerns."

Prayer is like a pressure reliever. You give your troubles and fears and concerns to God in prayer, and he is more than happy to take them.

"Where do the worries go for the people who don't pray?" Sharp said. "It's unbelievable to me, to leave those things to Him. That makes me think so much clearer and so much freer."

Pat's Perspective

I grew up in Wilmington, Delaware, and from the time I was a small boy, I attended church and Sunday school on a regular basis. I even went to a Baptist college, Wake Forest University, in North Carolina. However, it was not until I was twenty-seven years old that I realized that I wasn't a Christian and needed to make a decision to accept Jesus as my Savior and Lord.

I made that decision on February 22, 1968, in Spartanburg, South Carolina, and my life changed dramatically. For the first time I realized my sins had been pardoned and there really was a purpose for my life. God's peace flooded my soul and his power has undergirded me every day since.

As a Christian, my life has not been perfect. I have had many difficult experiences along with many triumphant moments. However, through it all the Lord has been the centerpiece of my life and has never left me or forsaken me.

I often tell young people that when you make a decision for Christ, he gives you an abundant life here on earth and an eternal life after you take your last breath. Everything we do on earth lasts for just a short time, but it gives us an opportunity to practice getting ready for our life in heaven where we will spend trillions of years.

That's an exciting way to live your life now and the first-class way to go into your forever life in heaven.

~

The Bible is my daily map. It's God's word.
There's so much wisdom there, that you
have to read it on a daily basis.

—Tim Salmon, Anaheim Angels

I confess my sins as I exhale, and I receive God's grace
and forgiveness with every inhalation.

—Bill Bright, founder of Campus Crusade for Christ

There's no way of knowing the peace that
comes from experiencing God's plan for your life,
until you recognize the importance of close,
consistent fellowship with Jesus Christ.

—Bob Estes, pro golfer

Whoever is on God's side is on the winning side
and cannot lose. Whoever is on the other side is on the
losing side and cannot win. Here, there is no gray area . . .
no gamble. There is freedom to choose which side
we shall be on, but no freedom to negotiate the
results of the choice, once it is made.

—A. W. Tozer, author and pastor

If you say you know Christ—without changing—
you should question who you know.

—Anne Graham Lotz, speaker and author

I didn't go to religion to make me happy.
I always knew a bottle of port would do that.
If you want a religion to make you feel really comfortable,
I certainly don't recommend Christianity.

—C. S. Lewis, author

As a Christian, I'm never surprised by vice.
I'm more surprised by virtue. Because of our inherent,
sinful nature, we are more prone to do the wrong thing
than the right thing. That's why we need God.

—Mike Cromartie, radio host

As the saying goes, there is no sinner without
a future, and no saint without a past.

—Chris Dodd, U.S. senator

God always has my best interest at heart,
and it's up to me to follow Him and look for
His direction in my life. If I do that,
everything else will take care of itself.

—Robbie Tobeck, Seattle Seahawks

My parents always taught me that
I was fortunate, that God had blessed me to give
me these opportunities, that you shouldn't take them
for granted, and that not everybody had them.

—Condoleezza Rice, U.S. Secretary of State

God is sovereign, even in things
we don't understand.

—Author unknown

Never tell a young person that anything
cannot be done. God may have been waiting
for that moment to see it happen.

—John Andrew Holmes, author

When you have nothing left but God,
for the first time, you become
aware that God is enough.

—Maude Royden, peace activist

Character takes years to form and a lifetime to prove.
I believe I'm still developing and proving
the image of the God I serve.

—A. C. Green, former NBA player

When you think about Jesus' life on Earth,
and what He did for us, it's the most beautiful thing that
ever happened, and there are no strings attached.

—Mike Holmgren, NFL coach

This is a short life . . . seventy to eighty years, at best.
To know that we will spend eternity in heaven with God,
because we put our faith in Christ, is the main promise
in the Bible. What more comforting thing can
there be, than to know your eternal destiny?

—Kyle Brady, Jacksonville Jaguars

*I wouldn't trade my position in Christ for a
thousand NBA championship rings, for a thousand
Hall-of-Fame rings, or for a hundred billion dollars.*

—Pete Maravich, former NBA star

*Nothing is or can be accidental
with God.*

—Henry Wadsworth Longfellow, poet

*A Christian can't lose. If we live, we go on
serving Him, and that's an adventure. If we die, we're
in heaven with Him, and that's incredible. Jesus is worthy of
every ounce of allegiance we can give Him . . . our love,
our devotion, our obedience and our trust.*

—Dr. Bill Bright, founder of Campus Crusade for Christ

*It's just fascinating how God opens up doors for you.
He just kind of maps you along where He wants you
to grow and learn and mature as a Christian.*

—Homer Drew, basketball coach, Valparaiso University

Faith is putting all your eggs in God's basket;
then, counting your blessings,
before they hatch.

—Ramona Carroll

Jesus says I love you just the way you are,
and I love you too much to let
you stay that way.

—Chris Lyons, pastor

Faith is like radar that sees through the fog . . .
the reality of things at a distance that
the human eye cannot see.

—Corrie Ten Boom, author

TWO

Dare to Dream

Dreams are to the soul what gasoline is to the engine. If the joy and delight of youth are to be forever yours, you must find a way to dream and hope, to believe in tomorrow. Since dreams are formed in the mind, this aspect of living life forever young means thinking right thoughts, being positive about life, and finding ownership in the here and now in order to directly affect tomorrow.

Professional golfer Jack Nicklaus believes that to make dreams come true, a person has to develop a reservoir of strength of body and mind. In Jack's mind, that reservoir has a name—attitude.

"Attitude is what carries you through the toughest times, when dreams are only dreams. And attitude is what enables you to enjoy your successes and not be carried away by them. To keep your attitude positive, you have to feed it with positive thoughts.

"I never lost the inherent belief that I could win, and that I could beat anyone and everyone. It didn't always translate into wins. But it always kept me in there. During a run of outs, it kept me thinking that my day would come. I would win again!"

How did things work out for Jack Nicklaus?

His positive attitude and determination to dream about tomorrow kept him young and enthusiastic about life and the game of golf. The results remain stunning—eighteen Majors and a hundred other tournament victories along the way. Impressive proof that dreaming—thinking right, believing in tomorrow—is one way to stave off the doldrums that come with growing old. Dreaming is one very good way to stay forever young.

It Doesn't Add Up

I was shopping in a health food store the other day when a little girl approached me.

"Buy a candy bar, mister?" She was maybe nine or ten years old, pale skin and bright red, curly hair. Her shabby clothes and tired eyes told a story that needed no words.

"Okay," I stopped and smiled at her. "What's the money go for?"

"We're building a park for the apartments a few blocks away." She squinted in the afternoon sun. "Buy a candy bar, mister? Please?"

Something about the girl tugged at me, her tone or maybe her eyes. I couldn't put my finger on it. For a moment I mulled over the idea of a new park cropping up near the apartments the girl referred to. I looked a few yards away at the white van and shady-looking characters restocking the candy for the young sales people.

I doubted the premise of the fundraiser, but I wanted to give the girl a sale. "Sure, honey." I dug through my pockets, but after a few seconds I came up with only a twenty-dollar bill. I shrugged. "Sorry. I only have a twenty."

"That's okay!" The little girl's smile didn't quite make it up to her eyes. "Just buy twenty candy bars, mister. They're a dollar each!"

I chuckled at her enthusiasm. "I'll tell you what." I rubbed my chin. "I think I have a better idea." I pointed to her money bag. "How much you got in there?"

She looked suddenly skeptical, but she sifted through the pouch. "A ten and four ones." She thought a minute. "Fourteen dollars."

"Okay, then." I held the twenty dollars out toward her. "I'll give you this, and you give me six candy bars and the fourteen dollars."

At first the girl grabbed the wad of bills from her bag and tentatively held them toward me. Then, in a rush she shoved them back inside and took three quick steps back. "If I do that I'll lose all my money!"

"No, honey, it's not like that." I shifted my position, thinking of a way to make it clear to her. "This is only one bill, but it's worth a lot more than all those bills in your bag."

The alarm on her face only grew. "No, mister!" She shook her head, backing up some more. "You want all my money, and I won't give it to you!" She turned around and ran back to the van, back to whatever leader had suckered her into selling candy bars for him.

As she clung tight to her money bag, I chuckled sadly. Aren't we just like the little redhead sometimes? We hold tight to what we know about today, the safe and sure, the tried and true. But we fear exchanging it for something bigger and better.

That kind of thinking doesn't add up! Young people need to be risk takers. Dream big. Dream now. Dream without limits! Dreams mean taking risks.

Through your school years you took risks joining clubs or teams, trying out for a spot on an athletic squad, taking the step to ask out a girl or talk to a boy. You ran easily, danced easily and dreamed easily. Keep that going if you want to live forever young.

Have an Espresso on Me

The young man was raised in the projects of Brooklyn in government-subsidized housing, while his father bent over backwards to make ends meet. He didn't get off to a good start, taking a series of dead-end jobs. Rather than being bitter and jaded about his place in life, the kid worked hard and relied on himself to succeed.

He left New York in his late twenties and took a job with a low-budget coffee bean supplier in Seattle. The youngster saw greater possibilities for the store, but the owners were satisfied with the status quo. Undaunted, he pushed them to expand beyond just coffee beans, to espressos and lattes.

They wanted nothing to do with that. Change was too much for them to imagine.

The kid's ambition drove him, and he finally left the coffee bean supplier for another job. But he didn't stop thinking about his ideas.

Today? Well, Howard Schultz is grown up. He has partners and offices and a place on the New York Stock Exchange. His stores are scattered throughout the country and around the world, the most successful national chain of coffee shops ever.

You know them as Starbucks.

Sold Short

Abraham Maslow said that the story of the human race is the story of men and women selling themselves short. Most people settle for far less than they are truly capable of, less than they might dream of accomplishing. Most people allow themselves to be convinced on the flimsiest of evidence that they lack the potential and ability of other people who are doing better than they are. They settle for mediocrity, rather than committing themselves to a dream for tomorrow, a future of excellence.

When you see Arnold Schwarzenegger, you do not dismiss his muscular development by attributing it to luck or genetics. He has worked for many years and invested thousands of hours to develop himself physically. Everyone starts with pretty much the same muscular structure Arnold Schwarzenegger started out with, as a skinny teenager growing up near Graz, Austria. The only difference is that Arnold Schwarzenegger has developed his muscles and the average person has not.

In terms of the ability to dream, to think positively, to imagine your potential, most people are quite similar.

"Everyone has the same brain structure," Maslow said. "Everyone has a variety of talents and abilities. Some people start off with greater natural advantages and personal endowments, but on an average, each person has the ability to develop far beyond anything he or she has achieved so far."

Once Upon a Time . . .

There once was a king who had two servants. To the first he said, "I want you to travel for six months through my kingdom, and bring back a sample of every weed you can find." To the second servant he said, "I want you to travel through my kingdom for six months, and bring back a sample of every flower you can find."

Six months later both servants stood before the king. To the first, the king asked, "Have you carried out my command?"

The first servant replied, "I have, and I was amazed to find there were so many weeds in the kingdom. In fact, our kingdom contains nothing but weeds."

The king then repeated the question to the second servant. "Have you carried out my command?"

The second servant replied, "I have, and I was amazed how many beautiful flowers there are in the kingdom. In fact, our kingdom contains nothing but beautiful flowers!"

Both servants found what they were looking for, and their success caused them to stop seeing anything else. Dreams are like that. Let God lead you to dream amazing things for your life. As writer Marcel Proust once said, "The only real voyage of discovery consists not in seeking new landscapes, but in having new eyes."

Hickory Dickory Dock

Author William Purkey tells a delightful little allegory concerning the value of feeling good about ourselves, the value of dreaming:

A mouse ran into the office of the Educational Testing Service, and accidentally triggered a delicate point in the apparatus, just as the College Entrance Examination Board's test was being scored for one young man named Harry Olson.

Harry was an average high school student who was unsure of himself and his abilities. Had it not been for the mouse, Harry's score would've been average or less, but the mouse changed all that. The scores that emerged from the computer were in the 800s, putting Harry in the top one percent in both the verbal and quantitative areas.

When the scores reached Harry's school, the word of his giftedness spread like wildfire. Teachers began to reevaluate their gross underestimation of this fine boy, and counselors trembled at the thought of neglecting such talent. College admissions officers began recruiting Harry for their schools.

New worlds opened for Harry and—as they opened—he started to grow as a person, as a student. Once he became aware of his potentialities and began to be treated differently by the significant people in his life, a form of self-fulfilling prophecy took place. Henry began to apply his mind to the great things of life. Ten years later—when the truth about the mouse and the wrong test scores came to light—Harry was a successful businessman and leader in his community.

The power of dreaming for tomorrow by believing in today? It cannot possibly be measured. Dreams belong to the young at heart!

Pretty as a Picture

As an All-American NFL defensive end for seven years, Bill Glass lockered next to Jim Brown, the greatest fullback who ever lived. One day in a game against the New York Giants, Brown gained 232 yards. Bill looked at his teammate and shook his head. "Jim, how did you gain 232 yards in one game? That's fantastic! How did you get yourself so 'up' to play?"

Jim Brown was hesitant with his answer. Finally he said, "All week long before we played against New York, I saw myself ripping up the middle, catching passes, making blocks, and doing everything I was going to do in the game, and when the game finally came and I did those things well, I wasn't surprised."

Isn't that all we're talking about?

It's a large point of success in athletics, and in life, to have vision and dreams, and to see yourself doing the thing you want to do. It's what you did through school! You pictured yourself acing the test, getting the girl or guy, having fun at the dance or football game. You thought it, saw it, believed it and did it.

A high percentage of athletes agree with Jim Brown. Oftentimes in the dugout, on the bench or on the ride to a game, athletes go over the game in detail—over and over and over again.

"Prior to the game," Jim says, "I imagined in vivid detail just what I would do in the game. It happened just as I imagined it would!"

Oh, the power of a dream!

Spaced Out

Actor Christopher Reeve, who died in October 2004, was a spokesperson for people with disabilities. He had much to say about daring to dream, about believing in tomorrow. While he was rehabilitating after the horseback riding accident that left him a quadriplegic, Reeve asked his nurse to pin a poster of the space shuttle on the wall. Every astronaut at NASA had signed the poster, offering Reeve the inspiration he needed to find his way out of that hospital room.

On top of the picture it said, "We found nothing is impossible."

Reeve believed that should be our motto in everything we dare to dream.

"So often our dreams seem impossible at first. Then they seem improbable. And finally, when we summon the will, they become inevitable," Reeve said. "If we can conquer outer space, we should be able to conquer inner space."

And inner space—the heart, mind and soul—is the place where dreams are born, where your positive thoughts take root, and your ability to believe in God's plans for your future will ultimately thrive.

Happy Dreams

Book publisher Sam Moore likes to make things simple for people.

"Let me speak plainly," he says. "People with a bad attitude usually end up losers. A positive attitude usually winds up winning. By nature some people tend to have a bad attitude. It may be stimulated by their background, their family, their failures, their upbringing. They often turn out to be losers. It is very hard to help them change their attitudes."

A positive attitude means daring to dream. If your attitude is strong and focused on the future, your dreams will be that much closer to reality.

Sam Moore offers some simple help when it comes to having the right attitude:

1. You are responsible for your attitude. People talk about inheriting their negative attitude from their parents. Only you can correct your attitude. The last of the human freedoms is to choose your own attitude, no matter what your circumstances.

2. The attitudes of leaders affect their followers. You can do a lot of good, just by being positive for those around you. Positive people have an infectious manner—and that blesses the whole company, team or family.

3. No one can have a good attitude all the time. Circumstances affect our lives. Make it your goal—as often as possible—to never say, "Well, under the circumstances . . ." Instead be on top of your circumstances. That's part of dreaming.

4. Be willing to change your attitude. When self-pity and a lackluster dream life become a part of your mind-set, recognize the fact. Then have the courage and strength to change your attitude. You'll be dreaming before you know it.

Don't Be a Walleyed Pike

Dr. James Dobson, founder of Focus on the Family ministries, tells a story about the walleyed pike, a large fish with an enormous appetite for minnows.

Something surprising happens when a plate of clear glass is slipped into a tank of water, placing the pike fish on one side and the minnows on the other. The pike can't see the glass, and repeatedly it will run smack into the glass barrier in pursuit of its dinner. Again and again and again the pike fish hits the glass, but eventually he stops going after the minnows.

The tiny fish are off-limits, unattainable, and so the walleyed pike gives up.

Here's the strangely sad part. At that point you can remove the plate of glass from the tank and allow the minnows to swim around their mortal enemy in perfect safety. The pike will not bother the minnows, and he will not even attempt to swim in their direction.

The walleyed pike knows what it knows—the minnows are unreachable.

At that point, the pike will actually starve to death while surrounded by abundant amounts of food.

Dream and dream and dream again. One of these days the obstacles in your way just might be removed. Don't be like the walleyed pike and give up just before the dream becomes possible.

Pat's Perspective

On June 15, 1947, I was seven years old. My dad took me to my first major league baseball game that day, a doubleheader between the Cleveland Indians and the Philadelphia Athletics. I was instantly captivated by the sights, sounds and smells of baseball. The next morning, I woke up with a dream planted in my mind. I wanted to be a major league ballplayer. I spent the next sixteen years working and preparing to make that dream a reality.

I never made it to the big leagues as a player, but after spending seven years as a minor league catcher and front office executive with the Philadelphia Phillies, I switched sports and joined the front office of the Philadelphia 76ers of the NBA in 1968. That started a career in the NBA, which now spans thirty-seven seasons.

Walt Disney once said, "If you can dream it, you can do it." Everything in life begins with a dream.

What are your dreams? How can you make your dreams become reality? Here are the steps you need to take as outlined by my wife, Ruth, who teaches for the Franklin-Covey Company. Answer the following questions:

1. Why? Why do you want to live that dream? What is driving you, motivating you? Your answer should be connected in some way to something of value to you in your life. My dream was connected to my love of sports. That value gave me the impetus to do what it took to get where I wanted to be.

2. What? What do you want to do specifically? Be very clear about your dream. The clearer the dream, the more likely it is to happen. So don't just dream that you want to go to college. What degree do you want? Where do you want to go to school? Dream in detail.

3. When? When do you want to complete the dream? What is your deadline? A dream without a deadline remains a someday forever and never happens. So put a date on that dream of yours.

4. How? How are you going to get there? What are the steps you need to take to make it happen? Break your dream into baby steps and just take one step at a time. And one day—you'll be living that dream of yours!

~

To have ideas is to gather flowers;
to think is to weave them into garlands.

—Anne-Sophie Swetchine, writer

The future belongs to those who see the possibilities,
before they become obvious.

—John Sculley, author

In reality, the only limitations on your abilities
are the ones that exist in your own mind.

—Brian Tracy,
motivational speaker

Just one great (dream) can completely
revolutionize your life.

—Earl Nightingale, author

*What you're thinking right now is influencing
every aspect of who you are.*

—Dr. Gladys McGarey, counselor

*The real winners in life are the people who
look at every situation with an expectation that they
can make it work, or make it better.*

—Barbara Pletcher, writer

*If you think there is a limit on what you
can accomplish, then there will be.*

—Richard C. Miller, teacher

*Six Words for Success—Think things through . . .
then follow through!*

—Edward Rickenbacker, former pilot

*I visualized where I wanted to be. I dreamed of what
kind of player I wanted to become. I knew exactly where
I wanted to go, and I focused on getting there.*

—Michael Jordan, NBA great

*I've learned from experience that the greater
part of our happiness or misery depends on our
dispositions and not on our circumstances.*

—Martha Washington, former first lady

*Great things are done by people who
think great thoughts and then go out into the
world to make their dreams come true.*

—Author unknown

*Man's mind, stretched to a new idea,
never goes back to its original dimensions.*

—Sir Oliver Wendell Holmes, Sr., author and physician

*Only those who dare to fail greatly
can ever achieve greatly.*

—Robert F. Kennedy, former U.S. senator

When life throws you a curveball, hit it!

—Criswell Freeman, author

Nothing on earth can stop the man
with the right mental attitude from achieving his goal;
nothing on earth can help the man with
the wrong mental attitude.

—Thomas Jefferson, former U.S. president

There is very little difference in people,
but that little difference makes a big difference.
The little difference is attitude. The big difference
is whether it is positive or negative.

—W. Clement Stone,
president of Combined Insurance

THREE

Live Healthy

Living life forever young requires attention to many areas in your life. But none will have so drastic an effect on you as your decision to take care of your health. Today, as you graduate, most of you are probably healthy. But this chapter will help you see the importance of maintaining your good health. If your health is failing, the following pages will give you suggestions to help improve it.

What areas make up your health? Take a hard look at the following:

- Avoidance of drugs and other abuses
- Diet
- Water intake
- Physical fitness
- Good sleeping habits

Ghastly Game

Years ago, in Tampa, Florida, three teens went home after school one day and smoked pot for a couple of hours. High and bored, looking for something to do, the three decided to steal traffic signs from their community and use them to decorate the walls of their bedrooms. An alligator crossing sign, maybe. A school zone sign, and finally a stop sign. An eclectic collection of stolen goods, something to satiate the appetites of a drug-induced stupor.

Within the hour, the signs were in the trailer where one of the teens lived. Laughing at their success, the teens smoked some more weed and joked about which of them would get which sign.

About the same time, four other teenagers were finishing soccer practice at the local high school. Typically, three of the four took rides home with one of their mothers. But that day the mother had other business, so all four climbed into the small two-door car belonging to the team captain, Randy. All four boys knew each other from church and honors classes. They were—as one teacher later said—the cream of the crop, the kids most admired by their teachers and peers.

With three extra passengers that afternoon, Randy took a different way home from school. When he came upon a busy intersection, he assumed he had the right-of-way because there was no stop sign saying otherwise. He traveled east into the intersection without reducing his speed and was instantly broadsided by a diesel truck headed south.

The wreck was horrific. All three of Randy's teammates died at the scene, and Randy died four hours later at the hospital. One of the last things he said to his weeping mother was, "Mom . . . there was no stop sign."

Police quickly found the teens who had stolen the stop sign that afternoon and arrested them. In a statement made to the judge and jury at a trial a year later, one of the teens said, "We were so wasted, I mean, we didn't know what we were doing. We actually thought it was cool to steal a stop sign. You know, cool to have a stop sign on our wall." He was crying as he spoke, and he stopped to wipe his eyes. "I guess it was the pot that made us so stupid."

Stupid and deadly.

Four kids snatched in the prime of life because of the ramifications of drug use. Drugs, partying . . . it's all stupid. If you want to stay forever young, don't touch the stuff.

Sober Up

The apostle Peter is under the inspiration of God when he puts up a huge warning sign in 1 Peter 5:8 with these two words: Be Sober!

Peter alerts us to the battle. The word *sober* literally means to build a defensive wall of protection around you and have an unclouded mind free from intoxicants. This referred to the huge ancient walls used to fortify and protect cities from harmful invaders. Likewise, the word *sober* indicates a sound, healthy mind, one that is able to guard and protect our thoughts.

The Scripture makes it clear that since our thoughts determine the direction of our lives, we cannot—must not—allow anything to capture our thoughts or to impair our judgment. If you've allowed drugs or alcohol to alter your ability to move ahead in life, even if you've allowed it to dull or darken a single day of your life, then take hold of this forever-young warning:

Sober up!

Cough Up the Coffin Nails

If you smoke cigarettes, here's the best advice you'll ever get: Stop! Stop immediately and never look back. This single habit will cost you more time, money, friends and good health than possibly any other.

Dr. John Tickell once said this: "You smoke? You're kidding me. The stuff that comes out of the back end of a cigarette is basically the same stuff that comes out of the back end of an automobile."

Carbon monoxide, hydrogen cyanide and other lethal chemicals make up what is basically a toxic mix. It's the same mix that smokers inhale every day. The average smoker smokes twenty cigarettes a day for thirty-five years. That's a quarter of a million cigarettes. There are ten puffs per cigarette, so that's 2.5 million puffs.

Dr. Tickell goes on to make these two statements about smoking:

• It is impossible to be intelligent and smoke at the same time.
• If your lungs were on the outside where everyone could see them, no one—absolutely no one—would think about smoking.

Babe's Greatest Error

Babe Ruth, one of baseball's all-time legends, made one very crucial error. He used smokeless tobacco. Yeah, sure, you or maybe some of your friends use it now. But if you want to go the distance feeling young, stay away from the snuff. When Babe Ruth died in 1948 he weighed just 137 pounds. The cause of death? A throat tumor caused by the smokeless tobacco. It was rumored that Babe would swallow the plug of chew and then gulp down a bicarbonate of soda to relieve the pain in his stomach. Think of all the records Babe Ruth set over the years. Too bad he never got past his fifty-third birthday to relive them. Learn from one of Babe's greatest errors—chewing tobacco. Don't chew.

Drop the Disease

Health expert Dr. Robert C. Atkins once said, "The American population is a diseased population." He goes on to say that most Americans are eating a totally unhealthy diet and have been eating so poorly all their lives that they accept poor health as the norm, unaware of how well they could really function by eating correctly.

"Our bodies literally become what we put into them," Atkins said. "In other words, if you put live food—fresh fruit, vegetables, nuts, grains and seeds into your body, you will lengthen your life.

"Likewise, if you eat dead food—foods with preservatives and additives, processed foods—you will diminish the quality of your life and hasten your death."

Atkins liked to ask people this question: "What did I eat today, that would grow if I planted it in the ground?"

Without proper nutrition, your body won't have the necessary building materials to properly replace worn tissues and sustain life. Remember this . . . you may have survived on mostly junk food until now, but you won't survive that way for long. The body is an amazing creation, knit together by God to withstand much of what is done to it over the years. Decades of a junk food diet will rob you of your youth.

If you choose to head into your "grown-up" years eating a steady diet of junk food, you will be killing yourself. If you eat the wrong kinds of food you might get by with it for a while, maybe even for a number of years. But the cumulative effect of that way of eating will eventually destroy you.

Eat smart. Start now.

Enough to Make You Sick

Here's a tally of what we eat, and what we spend on food or exercise equipment in the United States each day:

- We eat 75 acres of pizza.
- We eat 53 million hot dogs.
- We eat 3 million gallons of ice cream.
- We eat 3,000 tons of candy
- We drink 524 million servings of pop.
- We eat 2,739,726 donuts.
- We spend $3,561,644 on tortilla chips.
- We spend $10,410,959 on potato chips.
- Some 101,280,320 adults are on diets.
- We spend $2,021,918 on exercise equipment.

If you stop eating these junk foods, you'll be on your way to a forever-young life—and you'll feel a lot better along the way.

Super Foods

Most doctors and nutritionists agree that there are certain foods that contain more nutrition than others. It's important that your diet include the following foods, along with an assortment of lean proteins, fresh fruits and vegetables, nuts, seeds, legumes, and grains. But among those, these super foods should be eaten more often:

- Blueberries
- Lean turkey
- Soy products
- Raw almonds
- Grapefruit
- Flaxseed
- Broccoli
- Oats
- Plain yogurt

Eating Tips from Pam Smith

Bestselling author Pam Smith, who lives in Orlando, is a leading authority on good eating habits. Years ago when all of our children were at home, Pam helped feed them and offered nutritional advice. Here are her rules for good eating habits:

- Eat early. Your first meal should be when you get up in the morning, not in the middle of the day. Your body needs fuel to help start the day well.
- Eat often. You should be eating lots of small meals throughout the day rather than a few giant meals.
- Eat balanced. You must eat from the major food groups, which, by the way, do not include Twinkies and Krispy Kreme Donuts. You need to eat the right mix of protein and good carbohydrates, which includes fresh vegetables, fruit, grains and other healthy foods.

- Eat bright. The brighter and shinier the fruit and vegetables you eat, the better they are for you.
- Eat lean. Make sure you eat foods that are low in fat grams to help keep those extra inches off your body.
- Water is the beverage of champions, not Gatorade or Coca-Cola or iced tea.

Breakfast of Champions

Researchers examined the diets of Olympic athletes from more than 120 countries and discovered the food these athletes ate had three things in common:

1. The athletes ate a wide variety of good food, in order to receive a full spectrum of nutrients.
2. They ate a lot of lean-source protein. This is protein that is low in fat, such as fish, chicken and high quality beef or pork. Some of them were vegetarians who ate soy-based foods, but they all avoided fatty foods.
3. They drank lots of water. You need about one gallon of water per day to flush toxins from your body and keep it functioning at its best.

The All-You-Need-to-Know Diet

If you're going to keep the youth and vigor you enjoy today, you'll have to learn to control your weight. Only *you* can control your weight. It's a matter of being disciplined about what goes into your mouth.

Don't let excess weight and overeating rob you of a life meant to be lived to the full.

So what exactly should you be eating, and what should you be avoiding? If you're like most graduates, the past few years probably haven't been a shining example of dietary health. Now's the time to take control! You really don't need a bookcase of diet books to know how to eat correctly—author Brian Tracy breaks down the do's and don'ts of eating right with a few simple rules:

1. Eat more fruits and vegetables.
2. Eat lean proteins.
3. Eat lots of whole grain products.
4. Drink lots of water—at least one small glass per hour.
5. Avoid sugar.
6. Avoid salt.
7. Avoid white flour products.
8. Only eat when you're hungry.

Thirsty?

Most Americans do not drink enough water. This may not seem like a big problem now while you're in your late teens or twenties, but over time, dehydration will take its toll on every part of your good health. Take a look at these staggering statistics:

- Seventy-five percent of Americans are chronically dehydrated.
- In 37 percent of Americans, the thirst mechanism is so weak, it is often mistaken for hunger.

- Even mild dehydration will slow down one's metabolism as much as 3 percent.
- One glass of water shuts down midnight hunger pangs for almost 100 percent of the dieters studied in a University of Washington test.
- Lack of water is the number one cause of daytime fatigue.
- Preliminary research indicates that eight to ten glasses of water could significantly ease back and joint pain for up to 80 percent of suffers.
- A mere 2 percent drop in body water can trigger fuzzy, short-term memory, trouble with basic math, and difficulty focusing on the computer screen or on a printed page.
- Drinking eight glasses of water daily decreases the risk of colon cancer by 45 percent, breast cancer by 79 percent, and bladder cancer by 50 percent.
- When we are dehydrated, our appetite increases.

When we are dehydrated, rather than satisfy the true need of our body by drinking water, we often chase away the symptom with unnecessary food. There's a spiritual correlation to this as well. Jesus offers us living water, yet most of us are frequently dehydrated spiritually, as well. That feeling leaves us hungry for something to satisfy our souls, and we have a tendency to reach out for the wrong things.

It's time to drink from the water God gave us—to stave off false hunger in our bodies—and time to drink from the Living Water, to stave off false hunger in our souls. Jesus, the source of abundant and eternal life, is the giver of Living Water.

Feeling thirsty yet? Go get a drink of water right now. You can sip on the good stuff while you read on about staying forever young.

Seriously?

Broadcaster and author Bill O'Reilly says, "We all get one body, and most of us abuse the heck out of it. . . . We pour intoxicating pollutants into our bodies, we pierce and tattoo them, we gorge on terrible food, and then we don't go to the doctor to gauge the damage. It's insane."

O'Reilly adds that the average American today will live into their seventies. Now to you young graduates that may seem like forever. It's not. From the start of life we should all do our best to maximize our time on earth. That means staying healthy.

Then O'Reilly states, "I am simply astounded by people who smoke, drink heavily and ingest narcotics. Millions of us are abusing the one thing we have some control over. God gives you a body, a mind and a free will. He expects you to protect the franchise, but most of us don't."

Finally, O'Reilly reminds us that only you can look out for yourself: "If you are grossly overweight or underweight, don't bathe regularly, refuse to go to a dentist, or do a myriad of other things that will hurt your body, no one can do anything for you. You will pay a painful price, inevitably."

Better than a Horse? Of Course!

Dream for a minute that you're able to invest in a prize racehorse— a top racehorse that could cost you several million dollars.

Okay, now it comes time to feed the horse. What exactly would you feed your prize possession? Candy bars? French fries? Potato chips? Of course not! You'd buy the finest, freshest food around—anything to ensure that your investment is protected.

What about exercise? Would you allow your horse to stand around in his stall eating hay? Or would you follow an active regimen that built the horse's strengths and speed, one that helped the horse to stay heart-healthy?

Imagine the audacity of giving your racehorse tobacco or other drugs. And imagine depriving the horse of sleep or water. You'd never do it. The investment is simply too much to risk.

Now take a look in the mirror.

The body you see before you is one you can't buy again—not for any amount of money. You, dear graduate, are worth so much more than a racehorse at any price. You are a child of God, worth enough that Christ died on the cross so you could believe in him and find access to heaven.

With all that in mind, shouldn't you treat yourself at least as well as a horse?

Of course!

Get Some Shut-Eye

If you want to live like there's no tomorrow, if you want to keep the enthusiasm and youth of today, you must—absolutely must—get enough sleep. You need seven to eight hours of sleep each night for optimal performance. Yes, there'll be times when you need to pull an all-nighter. But if you fail to get at least six hours of sleep on a regular basis, you'll wind up with a sleep deficiency.

There is a pretty good chance you've been living that way for a few years now, because students are notorious for missing out on shut-eye. But as you enter the adult work-a-day world, sleep will become more and more important.

At least 60 percent of Americans exist with a sleep deficit, a weary feeling that will influence all your waking hours. These people go to bed too late, get up early, and go through the day feeling tired. You can't dance your way through life if you can't keep your eyes open. Here are four signs that you aren't getting enough sleep:

- Fog-like mental capacity
- Inability to function at your best
- Mentally slow
- Physically off balance

Do yourself a favor. Get the sleep your body needs. Develop the habit of getting to bed by ten o'clock each night, getting a good night's sleep, and having a day charged with energy to show for it. You might feel even younger than you do now!

Turn Off the Lights

Thomas Edison—the inventor of the light bulb—was big on keeping the lights off. He understood the importance of sleep, and he believed in taking naps. Legend has it that Edison didn't need much sleep. True he could survive on four or five hours of sleep each night, and he stayed up after everyone went to sleep.

In his study he had what he called a "thought bench." There he would sit in the utter quiet and reflect, thinking through his next move, his next idea. But during the day, as he tired, he would take naps. Sometimes his naps were only five or six minutes long, but the important thing was this: He got enough sleep.

Most people will do better to have seven or eight hours of sleep a night, and still maybe take a nap or two. As long as you realize—as Edison did—the importance of turning the lights off and getting your rest, you are on the right track.

Get Moving

If you want to maintain or find the type of body that will take you through life feeling young and fit, you'll need to get excited about exercising regularly. Two types of movement will help take you through life. The first is aerobic exercise—or the act of constant movement.

Aerobic activity helps strengthen your heart and keeps your metabolism working properly. Aerobics also releases endorphins that will help give you a positive outlook through the day. Most doctors and athletic trainers agree that a person should do at least thirty minutes of aerobic exercise four to five days per week.

The other type of activity is anaerobic, or strength training. Strength training involves working our muscles against resistance. Each muscle group should be worked out at least twice a week, with a forty-eight-hour recovery period between same-muscle workouts.

Here are some ways you might work aerobic exercise into your daily routine:

- Bicycle to work.
- Take early morning walks with a friend.
- Use a treadmill.
- Ride a stationary bike while watching your favorite show.
- Use an aerobic exercise tape that you enjoy.

Here are some ways you might work strength training into your daily routine.

- Join a gym and have a trainer put you on a workout plan.
- Purchase handheld weights so that you can develop your own routine at home.
- Purchase a single piece of resistance equipment, with which you can do a variety of strength-training exercises.
- Develop a pattern of calisthenics by doing sit-ups, push-ups, and lifting soup cans instead of weights.

Utta Pippig, the great marathon runner, said, "Life is movement. The person sitting on the couch, he's living dangerously."

Whatever you choose to do, you need to get moving! Don't wait... make a plan and get started. You'll be forever glad you did.

The Vanishing Muscle

Most doctors agree that your peak physical age is somewhere around your thirty-second birthday. After that point, if you don't move a certain muscle every forty-eight hours, it's disappearing.

In addition, the biggest way to keep calcium in your bones is to bang them on the ground—through exercise, of course. Calcium, too, will begin to leave the bones if they're not exercised four or five days a week. Take your bones for a walk and put them bones to use in an aerobic routine.

Whatever you do, don't sit still for more than forty-eight hours. If you do, there's a good chance you'll wind up a skinny bag of bent bones hunched over in a nursing home. That said . . . get moving and keep moving you entire life!

Self-Discipline—You've Got a Friend in Me

When it comes to your health, the enemy isn't self-discipline.

In fact, if you want to hold on to the youthful feeling of today, you'll have to make friends with self-discipline. The slim body? The healthy heart? The ease with which you run the track at school? Time will work against every aspect of your health, and in the process you will have to make a choice.

Fall to it or fight it.

If you allow the sedentary lifestyle to reduce your heart function, and the junk food of your cafeteria days to clog your arteries, you will certainly pay a price. As you get older, if you try to satisfy your body's desires with immediate gratification, the price will be your health and vitality later on.

By fighting the effects of time, with a regular exercise plan and deliberately healthy food choices, along with other health-conscious decisions, you'll pay a price, too. Delayed gratification requires the price of self-discipline, self-denial. But the rewards far exceed the cost.

That's why self-discipline is your friend.

Contrary to what some people mistakenly think, discipline is not a negative word, but a positive one. It is best understood not as an end in itself but as a means to a desirable end. Self-discipline is a necessary exercise needed to fulfill just about any goal. It requires denying the lesser to gain the greater.

There are no shortcuts.

Most of us want the achievement without first making the investment. We want the butter without first churning the cream. But remember this! Great achievements come only with the help of our friend—self discipline. Yes, self-discipline is a taskmaster. But it is a friend, all the same. To become self-disciplined, to keep the health you enjoy today, you must put out the effort again and again and again.

Deny the lesser to gain the greater.

Take a look at these synonyms for self-discipline:

- Preparation
- Development
- Exercise
- Training

Go the Distance

All the time and energy you'll put into a career or a family or a life of faith won't matter if you don't take care of your body. And that's going to take discipline.

Bill Hybels, pastor of Willow Creek Church near Chicago, says, "The rewards of discipline are great, but they are seldom immediate. When the world clamors for instant gratification and easy solutions, it is hard to choose the way of discipline instead. You will never build a walk with God, a marriage, a body or a bank account by obeying the world's law of instant gratification. Payday will come, in its own time, if you endure the pain and put your nose to the grindstone now."

Art Williams, insurance executive, says it's important to remember that your physical life counts, too. "Personal health is one of the most often ignored areas of life," Williams says. "Yet it's the one area that—if abused—can literally destroy the pleasure of all the others." He goes on to offer some of the best advice you'll ever get: A healthy diet is the single most important aspect of maintaining a healthy body. Over the years, we've been conditioned to eat a refined, high-fat, high-cholesterol, high-salt diet. "We eat fast foods, whatever is convenient, and our taste buds begin to crave things that are harmful to us, physically," Williams says. "There's abundant information today pointing to the error of our ways and educating us to a diet of mainly vegetables, fruits and natural grains."

Lather on the Sunscreen

One hot, sunny summer day after I graduated from high school, I was visiting my relatives in Stone Harbor, New Jersey. I got the bright idea to go visit my girlfriend at the time in Avalon, a mere eleven-mile jaunt up the beach. I took off in the middle of the day and eventually made it to Avalon, spent the afternoon, and then walked back. By the time I got back to Stone Harbor, I was burned to a crisp and spent the next week in bed recovering from my day in the sun.

Like most young people, then and today, a nice dark tan is viewed as really cool. Unfortunately, I learned the hard way that a dark tan destroys your skin and leads to melanoma, one of the deadliest forms of cancer.

After a brief bout with skin cancer a few years ago, I am now a believer. I never go out in the Florida sunshine without being covered with 40-proof sunscreen and I wear a hat as well. I encourage you to do the same. My doctor, Maxine Tabas, has told me that in the state of Florida, we have an epidemic of skin cancer. Forget the dark, rich tan and plan on living a long life.

Pat's Perspective

One of my goals in life is to live to be one hundred years old (I'm sixty-five now). In order to reach that goal, I'm constantly making decisions about my health. Here are some of them:

I have never smoked a cigarette, chewed tobacco, taken a drink of alcohol, or used drugs of any kind.

I will eat as much fresh fruit and vegetables as possible and stay away from any food that is not high in nutritional value.

I do not drink sodas and try to consume eight big glasses of water every day.

Every day I attempt to run, walk or cycle for at least one hour. (I have finished thirty-two marathons in the last nine years.)

I do my best to get at least seven hours of sleep at night and take a short nap in the afternoon when possible.

Life is not much fun if you're not feeling well. Take care of that body God gave you and it will serve you well for many years. Join me in setting goals for a long, healthy life. The older you get, the longer range your goals must be. Once you stop setting long-range goals, the dying process begins. Eat and drink right, work out hard, rest well, and I'll see you at the 100 year mark!

~

*An active mind cannot exist in
an inactive body.*

—General George Patton

*What we do on some great occasions will
probably depend upon what we already are.
And what we are will be the result of
previous years of self-discipline.*

—H. P. Liddon, author

*Sometimes the most urgent and vital thing you
can possibly do is take a complete rest.*

—Ashleigh Brilliant, writer

*The greatest pleasure one has is
keeping and feeling fit.*

—Amos Alonzo Stagg,
football coach who lived to be 103 years old

*Thousands of people have studied disease.
Almost no one has studied health.*

—Adelle Davis, nutrition expert

You can't play ball without sleep.

—Joe Pepitone, former New York Yankee

*Went to bed, went to sleep, and
did not worry any more.*

—Harry S. Truman's diary entry on April 12, 1945,
the evening after taking the oath of office on the death
of President Franklin D. Roosevelt

Discipline yourself and others won't need to.

—John Wooden, former UCLA basketball coach

Go to bed. What you're staying
up for isn't worth it.

—Andy Rooney, CBS broadcaster

A disciplined person is one who follows the
will of the one who gives the orders.

—Vince Lombardi, former NFL coach

It's easier to maintain good health than
to regain it once it is lost.

—Dr. Kenneth Cooper, nutritionist and author

No man is free who is not
master of himself.

—Epictetus, Greek philosopher

There is only one kind of discipline:
perfect discipline.

—General George Patton

Without enough sleep we all become
tall two-year-olds.

—JoJo Jensen, *Dirt Farmer Wisdom*

The successful person makes a habit of
doing what the failing person
doesn't like to do.

—Thomas Edison, inventor

I cannot consent to place in the control of others,
one who cannot control himself.

—General Robert E. Lee

I've realized that most of my best ideas
have followed a good night's sleep.

—Thomas Edison, inventor

Health is the first muse, and sleep is the
condition to produce it.

—Ralph Waldo Emerson, poet

You've got to work at living . . .
99 and 9/10ths of Americans work at dying!
You've got to eat right, exercise and have goals and
challenges. Exercise is king; nutrition is queen.
Put 'em together, and you've got a kingdom.

—Jack LaLanne, fitness expert, at age ninety

FOUR

Don't Give Up

You've probably already faced failure in one way or another. Maybe during your school years failure seemed to be the worst thing you ever dealt with. But if you're going to live a youthful life, you'll discover that failure can be the best thing that ever happened to you.

It is only in the failing that we realize what we are made of, how strong a faith we really have. The Lord allows us a certain number of failures simply to teach us how to overcome. And overcoming is another key to living life forever young.

Make a decision that whatever you and God decide is your dream, you will keep on pushing for it. Don't ever give up!

Never Say Never—
Seven Who Didn't Give Up

Sometimes it helps if we know that the big names, the tried and true, the famous in our midst had their struggles too. In the next twenty years, you're bound to have a door or two shut in your face.

Not everyone will love your ideas, and some may even laugh. But if you can stay positive in the midst of that type of pain, you never know where you might wind up. Take a look at these seven people who refused to give up:

1. **Elvis Presley**—Presley earned a C from his music teacher at L. C. Humes High School in Memphis, Tennessee. The reason? She told him he couldn't sing. Presley, of course, went on to become the king of rock 'n' roll. He sold more than 600 million copies of his albums and singles. Before his death in 1977, he starred in thirty-three movies—singing in most of them.

2. **The Beatles**—The rock group that shook the universe was rejected in 1962 by Decca Records executive, Dick Rowe. Rowe, in a decision he would replay for the rest of his life, listened to first The Beatles, then the group Brian Poole and the Tremeloes. After very little time on the matter, Rowe signed Brian Poole and the Tremeloes. The Beatles were then turned down by four more major recording studios before being signed to a contract.

3. **Fran Tarkenton**—The great NFL quarterback Tarkenton made 2,781 incomplete passes during his professional football career. The good news? He set the NFL record for most passes completed (3,686), most yards passing (47,003), and most touchdown passes (342).

4. **Katie Couric**—The famous *Today Show* anchor was banned from reading news reports on the air by the president of CNN,

who allegedly claimed Couric had an irritating, high-pitch, squeaky voice. Couric worked with a voice coach and later was hired by the *Today Show*. The rest is history.

5. **Willie Nelson**—The famous country music singer sold encyclopedias and vacuum cleaners after his frustrations at not making a successful run at either country music or pig farming. Nelson decided to take another go at the country music business and soon wrote his first hit song, followed by a string of others. He says he learned priceless lessons selling door-to-door to make a living. It gave him time to think about how to do things differently in country music. Looks like the thinking paid off.

6. **John Grisham**—The bestselling novelist's first book, *A Time to Kill* was rejected by sixteen agents and a dozen publishing houses. Wynwood Press published 5,000 copies of *A Time to Kill* in 1989, but sales were almost nonexistent. Grisham kept on, producing his next title, *The Firm,* which was picked up by Dell Publishing and sold millions of copies. Two years later, Dell republished *A Time to Kill* and in 1996, it was made into a major motion picture.

7. **John F. Kennedy**—The former U.S. president failed to make the football team at the Canterbury School, his Connecticut prep school. A few years later, he bombed in his bid for president of his freshman class at Harvard University. In fact, he even missed out on his attempt to make student council. To top off his academic career, Kennedy dropped out of Stanford University Business School. But he didn't give up.

Go with the Flow

Sometimes failure happens because of something you did or didn't do. Other times life takes a left turn when you were headed right, and you're left with a failure you had nothing to do with.

Poet Robert Frost said he could sum up everything he learned about life in three words: It goes on! Frost said, "I believe that's oh so true! The human spirit can survive pain, loss, death, taxes and even wet panty hose, and life goes on and on and on."

The trick to staying forever young is to absorb the blow and learn from it—even if it wasn't your fault. You will never experience the benefits of failing if you spend too much time feeling angry at something you feel is unfair.

"Life is full of unforeseen detours. Circumstances happen which seem to completely cut across our plans," author Steve Penny once said. "Learn to turn your detours into delights. Treat them as special excursions and learning tours. Don't fight them or you will never learn their purpose. Enjoy the moments and pretty soon you will be back on track again, probably wiser and stronger because of your little detour."

Focus on that. You'll be wiser and stronger because of your experiences—whether you expected them or not.

Pass the Peanut Butter

Think about this the next time you eat a peanut butter sandwich. George Washington Carver, one of the most influential African-Americans in America's history, was an educator and innovator of agricultural sciences. He graduated from Iowa State College of Agriculture and Mechanic Arts in 1894. Two years later, he became director of the Department of Agricultural Research at what is now Tuskegee University in Alabama. At the university, he worked arduously on an exhaustive series of experiments with peanuts. Carver wrote articles and spoke often to farmers about the need to rotate crops, in order to keep from depleting the nutrients in the soil.

Only a handful of people paid attention.

Then, in 1902, the boll weevil migrated to Texas bringing with it devastating damage to the area's cotton crop.

"The boll weevil is not to be messed with," Carver told the farmers. "It's coming this way."

Carver laid out a plan for farmers to help them prepare for the boll weevil. The plan was this: If they planted peanuts and sweet potatoes, the spread of the boll weevil would be stopped. In addition, those crops would replenish the soil's nutrients. Still, most people continued growing only cotton.

Like clockwork, the boll weevil did come to Alabama. It munched its way across Texas, Louisiana and Mississippi. It finally arrived in Alabama just as Carver predicted. In 1914, Alabama's crops were completely ruined. Every crop grown at Tuskegee, except the peanuts and sweet potatoes, that is.

Finally the farmers sat up and took notice of Carver.

Whoops!

Because of Carver's warnings, farmers started to plant peanuts, but something unexpected happened. Yes, the boll weevil was stopped in its tracks. But Carver had underestimated a crucial part of the plan. There were so many peanuts now, that the price of peanuts fell sharply.

Carver was deeply disturbed.

He felt personally responsible for the financial ruin of every farmer who had taken his advice. Wherever he went, he was blamed for the colossal mistake. Not long afterward Carver disappeared to his lab—mostly to avoid the criticism from former friends and students. There he did something many modern-day scientists don't often do—he prayed. He said, "Help me, God. All the trouble is my fault. Give me wisdom about what to do next."

In a week's time, Carver had the sudden inspiration that maybe—just maybe—there were other ways to use the abundance of peanuts. Peanut butter, for instance.

Carver's horrible mistake and the research inspired by it, eventually resulted in more than three hundred derivative products from peanuts. What did Carver do? When faced with failure he took peanuts and made peanut butter. Over the next half century, peanuts became the sixth leading crop in the United States, and the second largest in the South.

Next time you reach for the peanut butter, remember George Washington Carver. Lying in the midst of every mistake is a way to turn peanuts into peanut butter. By keeping that type of positive attitude, you'll stay young at heart and never have a shortage of peanut butter sandwiches.

Dear Ann's Best Advice

One way to handle failure is to have the right attitude about failing before it ever happens. You must develop a mind-set that whatever comes your way—with God's help—you can get through it.

Advice columnist Ann Landers was often asked what one piece of advice was her most helpful. Her answer deals directly with the idea of failure: Expecting failure and knowing how to handle it when it comes.

Landers' response was, "Expect trouble as an inevitable part of life and, when it comes, hold your head high, look it squarely in the eye and say, 'I will be bigger than you. You cannot defeat me.'"

Take it from Ann Landers, with your faith firmly in place you can handle whatever comes your way. You better believe it!

Way to Go, Roy

On New Year's Day, 1919, Georgia Tech played the University of California in the Rose Bowl in Pasadena, California. It was the biggest game of the season for both teams. Shortly before halftime, a player named Roy Riegels recovered a fumble for California. In the confusion of the moment, he tucked the ball to his side and headed like the wind for the end zone.

The wrong end zone.

Ten yards, twenty, thirty—Roy led an entire field of players chasing him. What he didn't know was that those were his own players. Finally, one of his teammates tackled him just before he would've scored a touchdown for the opposing team. When California tried to punt on the next play, Georgia Tech blocked the kick and scored a safety.

Time wound down and the team filed off the field toward the locker room for halftime. The California players slumped into the room, deeply discouraged, but Roy was way beyond that. He put a blanket around his shoulders, put his face in his hands, and wept.

Coach Nibbs Price was quiet as he watched the scene. Just before the halftime break was over, Coach Price looked at the team and said, "Men, the same team that played the first half, will start the second."

Every player stood and filed out of the locker room except one— Roy Riegels. The coach called to him again, but still he didn't move. Finally, Coach crossed the room and said, "Roy, didn't you hear me? The same team starts the second half."

Roy looked up, tears in his eyes, and said, "Coach, I can't do it! I've ruined you, my school, myself. I couldn't face that crowd in this stadium right now to save my life."

Coach Price reached out, put his hand on Roy's back and said, "Roy, get up and go back. The game is only half over."

Roy later said that something welled up in him at the coach's words. The man was right—the game was only half over. He stood, shook the coach's hands, and sprinted back out to the field.

What happened next? Everyone who saw that famous game said it was the greatest half of football a player ever had.

That's how it'll be for everyone who wants to live life forever young. Yes, there will be mistakes and hard times. But the person who can stay positive, who can look at a situation and say, "It isn't over yet!" is the person who will hold on to the fire of life, the enthusiasm for tomorrow. After all, we're talking about second chances.

And second chances are only found if you look for them.

At Ease, Soldier

Most people who go through basic training in the army never forget their first day. From early morning to well after dark, recruits do nothing but run and do push-ups and sit-ups. By the end of the day, most people find they can barely stand, and that their arms and legs are shaking hard.

At that point, basic training feels like a cruel and unusual form of torture. Recruits glance at each other as if to say, "We volunteered for this?" The idea of waking in the morning and doing it all over again is more than the mind or body can fathom.

One day after another, the basic training time begins to pass. Running becomes second nature, sit-ups and push-ups can be done with relative ease. As that happens, something unusual takes place. Soldiers in training begin to look back at that first day and realize it was one of the best days of their lives. Not because of the workload and pain, not because they were drained emotionally and physically. That single day taught them more about themselves than they'd learned in a lifetime up to that point. The most common thing a recruit will say about the first day of basic training is this: "I never knew what I was capable of doing. From now on I'll look at life's challenges differently, knowing that I can handle much more than I thought I could."

Look at life's difficulties that way! Endure, make your way through them, and learn something about yourself—you are capable of far more than you ever imagined.

Easy as One-Two-Three

Inventor Charles Kettering says that all people must learn to fail intelligently. He said, "Once you've failed, analyze the problem and find out why. Because each failure is one more step leading up to the cathedral of success. The only time you don't want to fail is the last time you try."

Kettering gave these three points for turning failure into success:

1. Honestly face defeat—never fake success.
2. Exploit the failure—don't waste it. Learn all you can from it.
3. Never use failure as an excuse for not trying again.

Do this and you can truly live out the Scripture from James 1 that tells us to consider it pure joy when we suffer through many trials, because the suffering develops perseverance and perseverance helps to complete us in every way. Author Truman Capote put it a little bit differently when he said, "Failure is the condiment that gives success its flavor."

So, next time you fail, put a positive spin on it. Work on these three steps. Be honest. Learn. And always try again.

Say What?

The year was 1946 and musician Ray Charles got word that Lucky Millinder's band was coming to Orlando for a show. Ray did everything he could to get Lucky's attention, and finally he earned himself an audition with the band, a band that made records Ray loved listening to! It was the greatest break in young Ray's life, and he could hardly wait for the day of the audition. When it came, he walked in, seated himself at the piano and began to perform—singing and playing with everything he had.

Millinder sat quietly listening, and at the end of the audition, Ray Charles knew without a doubt that he had done his very best. He waited for the words of praise from Millinder, but they never came. Instead, the famed musician of that day made a slight coughing noise.

"Ain't good enough, kid."

The words were such a shock they stunned Ray. He could barely breathe as he asked Millinder the hardest question of his career to that point. "What did you say?"

Millinder was adamant this time. "You heard me. You don't got what it takes."

Ray Charles felt the pain of that criticism years afterwards. "I went back to my room and cried for days," he said.

But tears and disappointment for the graduate with a positive outlook can make all the difference. Of course, the late Ray Charles will always be respected as one of the most talented entertainers of all time, selling out shows and venues across the world whenever he performed.

What did Ray Charles say about that time in his life? "It was the best thing that ever happened to me. After I got over feeling sorry for myself, I went back and started practicing. That way no one could ever say that about me again."

Pat's Perspective

As I study the lives of successful men and women, I have noticed one common theme about their lives. They have all had many setbacks, disappointments and failures, but they never quit. No matter how difficult their circumstances, they all refused to give up.

Michael Jordan was cut by the varsity coach as a high school sophomore, but he didn't quit playing basketball. Derek Jeter, the Yankees' shortstop, said, "If Michael had quit, they wouldn't have named a shoe after him."

Winston Churchill, England's prime minister during World War II, failed many times as a young man and battled health problems as well. He was doggedly persistent his whole life and at one point said, "The bulldog's nose is pointed upward so he can breathe while holding on."

Pepper Rodgers, longtime college football coach, once told me, "When I was a sophomore quarterback at Georgia Tech, I got hurt. As a junior, I lost my job, but I hung in there and as a senior, I played on a team that went to the Orange Bowl. I wasn't a great player, but I was great at not quitting."

That's a powerful statement. You may never reach the top of your profession, but if you stick with it and keep persevering, you've already achieved the greatest reward. Let's all be good at not quitting!

~

Those who are the happiest are not necessarily
those for whom life has been easiest.

—Author unknown

Emotional stability is an attitude.
It is refusing to yield to depression and fear,
even when black clouds float overhead. It is improving
that which can be improved and accepting
that which is inevitable.

—Dr. James Dobson, founder of
Focus on the Family

Oysters use the sand-grain
irritant to make the treasured pearl.
Life asks this of you and me.

—Dorothy Corkille Briggs, author

Some people are always
grumbling because roses have thorns.
I am thankful thorns have roses.

—Alphonse Karr, writer

*No matter how dark things seem to be or
actually are, raise your sights and see the possibilities . . .
always see them, for they are always there.*

—Norman Vincent Peale, minister

*People are not remembered by how
few times they fail, but by how often they succeed.
Every wrong step is another step forward.*

—Thomas Edison, inventor

*Every great mistake has a halfway moment . . .
a split second when it can be recalled
and, perhaps, remedied.*

—Pearl S. Buck, writer

*If you want to increase your success rate,
double your failure rate.*

—Thomas Watson, Sr., founder of IBM

My downfall raises me to infinite heights.

—Napoleon Bonaparte, emperor of France

You may be disappointed if you fail,
but you are doomed if you don't try.

—Beverly Sills, opera singer

Mishaps are like knives that either serve us
or cut us, as we grasp them by
the blade or the handle.

—James Russell Lowell, poet

If you haven't failed,
you haven't tried very hard.

—Shirley Hufstedler, executive

In the middle of every difficulty,
lies opportunity.

—Albert Einstein, physicist

*I will tell you that there have been
no failures in my life. There have been no failures,
but there have been some tremendous lessons.*

—Oprah Winfrey, talk show host

*Suffering will come, trouble will come . . .
that's part of life, a sign you are alive.*

—Mother Teresa

*Too many victories weaken you.
The defeated can rise up stronger than the victor.*

—Muhammad Ali, boxer

*Many of life's failures are people
who did not realize how close they were
to success when they gave up.*

—Thomas Edison, inventor

Think not of yourself as the architect of your career,
but as the sculptor. Expect to have to do
a lot of hard hammering, chiseling,
scraping and polishing.

—B. C. Forbes, business leader

Life can be real rough . . .
you can either learn from your problems or
keep repeating them over and over.

—Marie Osmond, entertainer

FIVE

Work Hard and Happy

Think about how many times through the course of your school days someone told you to work hard. No matter how many times you heard those words, you didn't hear them often enough.

Why? Because hard work is another benchmark of living life forever young. Work hard and you'll go through life without any regrets. A group of home-school parents in Washington State have just two words as their credo: Work hard. That way when you're finished with the day you'll feel:

- Fulfilled
- Competent
- Strong
- Tired

If you're like most people your age, you reach that last benefit and your heels make a screeching sound against the pavement. Who wants to be tired, right? No one, not in the traditional sense. Not in the way so many adults walk through life, depressed, perplexed and frazzled.

But there's a different sort of tired, a tired that feels wonderful to the heart, mind and body. Even to the soul. That's the kind of sweet soul-stirring tiredness that comes after a day of honest, hard work. The Bible has something to say about working hard. Colossians 3:23 (NIV) says, "Whatever you do, work at it with all your heart, as working for the Lord, not for men."

And written between the words of that truth is an element of living life forever young, the element that involves not only working hard, but staying happy while you're at it. In other words, do the work, and love what you're doing.

Learn from the Ant

Highly acclaimed speaker and author Jim Rohn offers the "ant philosophy":

1. Ants never quit. If they are headed somewhere and you try to stop them, they'll look for another way.

2. Ants think winter all summer. Why do we need that advice? Because it's important to be realistic. In summer you've got to think "storm"; you've got to think rocks as you enjoy sand and sun. Think ahead.

3. Ants think summer all winter, reminding themselves that this won't last long; we'll soon be out of here. This applies to leadership skills. Average people look forward to getting off work, while successful people look forward to getting on with it.

4. How much will an ant gather during summer to prepare for winter? All that he possibly can.

The Real Shaq Attack

NBA superstar Shaquille O'Neal learned more about getting things done, more about working hard, from his mother than all his coaches combined.

"My mother had a different way," O'Neal says. "She was strong, like my father, but she was gentle, too."

O'Neal's mother told him that he must fulfill his dreams now, while there was still time. She told him he had to attack with a full head of steam. With Shaq still listening intently, she would add something more. "There's no opportunity like now," she told him. "This is the time when you can show people."

"I didn't feel like I could stand out among those other players," he says. "I tried to brush her off and tell her I couldn't do that right now, maybe later."

Shaq's mom would have nothing to do with that type of logic. She told him that later doesn't always come to everyone.

And those words were the ones that finally got to Shaquille O'Neal. *Later doesn't always come to everyone.*

"Those words snapped me into reality and gave me a plan. You work hard, now. You don't wait. If you're lazy or you sit back and you don't want to excel, you'll get nothing. If you work hard enough, you'll be given what you deserve."

Shaq says everything got easier for him after that. Attitude promoted a Shaq attack!

Whatever You Do

For thousands of years, laziness was considered a sin. And sure enough, the Bible's book of Proverbs tells us that if a man doesn't work, he shouldn't eat. In addition, there are dozens of verses on the ill effects of being idle.

It only makes sense that God's direction is good for us—whatever he leads us to do, we must work at with all our hearts.

Evangelist Billy Graham was raised in an environment where hard work was among the best things a person could do. To say a person was a hard worker was the highest compliments that could possibly be paid.

"I was taught that laziness was one of the worst evils, and that there was dignity and honor in labor," Graham once said. "I could abandon myself, enthusiastically, to milking the cows, cleaning out the latrines and shoveling manure. Not because they were pleasant jobs, but because sweaty labor held its own satisfaction."

This mind-set paid off in everything Billy Graham did. He was able to connect the idea that hard work was the same as diligence, and diligence was one of the traits of godliness. A diligent person will work hard at every task—no matter how important or mundane. Every effort is his best effort. Yes, he may feel tired at times, but that doesn't change his determination. He may feel sluggish, but he will never be a sluggard.

Hard work means that a man will be ruled by discipline, not emotions or transient feelings. Practicing diligence or hard work is one very good way to stand out for Christ.

It worked for Billy Graham.

"I Love Everything"

Florida State football coach Bobby Bowden once said this about life: "I haven't lost a drop of enthusiasm. I still can't wait to wake up in the morning and get going.

"I love to be out on the field, coaching our players.

"I love the strategy.

"I love to study film and find some weakness in an opponent that we might exploit.

"I love the excitement of game day.

"I love everything!"

Bowden couldn't imagine a life where a person didn't love the work he was given, or where a person wasn't determined to be happy while he was working hard.

"I've heard people talk about getting high on some of that funny dust or high on that goofy weed or high on alcohol," Bowden said. "I've never had the slightest temptation to use any of that stuff. Man, I can't imagine a greater high than the feeling of standing on the sidelines during an exciting game, with 60,000 people in the stands. I get goose bumps just thinking about it."

What is it you love to do? Find a way to make that a part of your life forever! And smile while you're doing it, because life is good.

Fight to the Finish

Working hard at the start is a pretty common practice. All of the runners in a long-distance race blow off the starting line. Halfway through the event you'll find the ones who worked hard in the months leading up to the race. Halfway through you'll also find the ones who didn't prepare well enough, didn't work hard.

Recently, Olympic swimmer Nancy Hogshead had the chance to speak to a large crowd. There, she spoke openly about the hard work she had to employ in order to be a champion.

"My parents knew nothing about swimming," Hogshead said, "but they knew a lot about not quitting."

Hogshead's parents told her that what she started, she would also have to finish, because she would either face the pain of discipline or the pain of regret.

There are lots of reasons to quit something. Maybe you were tricked into making the decision, or maybe all the facts weren't laid out for you to analyze. But hard work is not a reason to quit. It never will be. Every time you get into something, it's going to take hard work, whether it's another sport, going to college, a new job or having children.

Go through life the way Nancy Hogshead still does. Fight to the finish.

Count the Cost

From where you're standing today, with your diploma freshly framed on the wall, your dreams are bigger than life. That's a good thing. Having dreams is part of living life forever young. But have you considered what price you'll have to pay in order to earn that success?

Kathy R. Caulton, a writer and publisher, says when you are looking into your future, it's important to know which questions to ask. You don't need to ask, "Do I have what it takes to be successful?" The key question is, "Am I willing to pay the price for the success I desire?"

The price is always hard work. As you get older, you'll be tempted to think that overworking yourself is the equivalent of hard work. It's not that at all. If you're assigned to an eight-hour workday, keep your day to eight hours. Hard work does not mean staying at the office an extra hour or two every day, although sometimes you will have to work extra hours.

But within those eight hours, work hard. Give everything to that position, to the intellectual, physical and emotional challenges that the job demands from you. That's hard work, and that's the price you'll pay to realize your dreams.

Keep that in mind the next time you think of your dreams. And don't ever think hard work is too great a cost to pay for making your dreams come true. Remember, hard work will help keep you young while you're on your way.

Parting Words

Today you stand at the beginning of your adult life. Yes, you know something about hard work, because you managed to work your way through school and to graduate. Good for you. Now the real work can begin—a sort of work that must be hard and happy all at the same time.

Sometimes the best wisdom on how to approach hard work comes from those who have worked hard through the decades and now stand on the threshold of retirement. Take store manager Margaret Beans, a woman who ran a successful retail shop for thirty years. Beans wasn't famous and she won no awards or honors. But her hard work made her a pillar in her community.

On the day of her retirement party, Beans was commended for being loved by her family, friends, customers and community. When she had a chance to speak to the people gathered on her behalf, Beans offered a few parting words that all of us would do well to remember. This is what she said:

- Belong to something bigger than yourself.
- Work with others toward a common goal.
- Do your part.
- Take pride in doing your job well.
- Work hard to make your ideas take shape.
- Help build something of lasting value.

It is a sobering thought that we must continually keep proving ourselves all through our working lives. Rare is the person who can sit back and rest on past achievements. Basketball coach Tex Winter said, "You are only a success at the moment that you do a successful act." We often work toward a certain goal, thinking that when we reach that goal we will have it made. But it never works that way.

Hard work is a day in, day out sort of venture. The final bit of wisdom from Margaret Beans was perhaps her most profound thought of all:

"Every job completed is a new one begun."

A Commitment to Excellence

Former Green Bay Packer coach Vince Lombardi was well known for his demand that everyone working for him must have a commitment to excellence.

"If you give me anything less than your best, you're not only cheating yourself, your coaches, your teammates and everyone in Green Bay," Lombardi would say. "You're also cheating the Maker who gave you that talent."

"The heart of Vince Lombardi's philosophy as a coach was that every player on his team be committed to excellence," Bart Starr, former Green Bay quarterback, once said. "Every player had to do his best, to use his God-given talent to the fullest."

For Coach Lombardi there was no other way for his team to succeed. Lombardi liked to tell his players, "The quality of any man's life is in direct proportion to his commitment to excellence."

As you set out on the journey of life, be committed to excellence by making a constant check on your work habits. Are you giving your all to your work and career? If not, remember Vince Lombardi's words. And remember that it was Jesus Christ who first called us to excellence when he said, "Be ye perfect even as your heavenly Father is perfect."

Standing Ovation

Studies show that average adults put only about 25 percent of their effort into any given job. "The world takes off its hat to those who put in more than 50 percent of their capacity," Andrew Carnegie once said.

And the world will give a standing ovation to those few-and-far-between souls who devote 100 percent.

Pat's Perspective

A number of years ago, when my daughter Karyn was seventeen years old, I had a speaking engagement at a luncheon in Minneapolis. After I completed my talk, a man asked if he could drive me to the airport because he had an issue to discuss with me. As we were driving along, the man said, "My son is in the ninth grade and loves basketball. He wants to attend the University of Minnesota on a scholarship."

I replied, "That sounds terrific! What's the problem?"

The man answered, "Well, he doesn't want to do all the work in advance if he's not assured of getting the scholarship."

That answer staggered me. So when I got home, I told Karyn what happened and asked her, "Is that how people your age really are thinking?" Karyn said, "I hate to tell you this, Dad, but a lot of my friends don't want to do the work unless they know that they'll be rewarded."

Let me make this clear. The work always comes first and the rewards come as a result of it. In other words, there ain't no such thing as a free lunch! You have to put shoe leather to the pavement every day for the rest of your life. You *have* to work hard!

The two most important words in the English language are *what else*. In every situation ask yourself: *What else can I do? What else can I bring? What else can I offer?* If you are a *what else* kind of person, your services will always be in high demand.

~

Standing is harder than moving.

—Moshe Feldenkrais, philosopher

*When I am asked by young people for
the secret of success, I try to make them understand
that there is no mystery about it. The answer is
summed up in two words—work hard.*

—J. C. Penney, retailer

*It's okay to retire from a job, but you
should never retire from work.*

—Pat Williams, author

*Striving for success, without hard work,
is like trying to harvest where you haven't planted.*

—David Bly, author

*Work spares us from the three great evils—
vice, boredom and need.*

—Voltaire, writer

I can't imagine a person becoming a success,
who doesn't give this game of
life everything he's got.

—Walter Cronkite, broadcaster

When work is a pleasure, life is a joy.
When work is a duty,
life is slavery.

—Maxim Gorky, writer

In business or in football, it takes
a lot of unspectacular preparation to
produce spectacular results.

—Roger Staubach, after leading the Dallas Cowboys
to the Super Bowl Championship

The harder you work, the harder
it is to surrender.

—Vince Lombardi,
former NFL coach

Life doesn't require that we be the best,
only that we try our best.

—H. Jackson Brown, author

My father believed and taught me
that opportunity is just hard work in disguise.

—J. C. Watts, Jr., former U.S. congressman

I do the best I know how, the very best I can, and
I mean to keep doing so until the end.

—Abraham Lincoln, former U.S. president

If the power to do hard work is not talent,
it is the best possible substitute for it.

—James A. Garfield, former U.S. president

What people don't recognize is, if you outwork the
opposition, you put a better product on the field.

—Reggie Jackson,
former major league baseball star

My father used to tell me there are
two kinds of people, the takers and the givers.
"The takers sometimes eat better," he would say,
"but the givers always sleep better."

—Actress Marlo Thomas,
daughter of actor Danny Thomas

There will never be a system invented which
will do away with the necessity for work.

—Henry Ford, inventor

The world is full of willing people.
Some willing to work, the rest
willing to let them.

—Robert Frost, poet

When you win an award, set it in the lobby.
Then go back to work.

—Pat Williams, author

If you'll not settle for anything less than your best,
you'll be amazed at what you can
accomplish in your lives.

—Vince Lombardi, former NFL coach

When I was young, I observed that
nine out of every ten things I did were failures.
So I did ten times more work.

—George Bernard Shaw, playwright

Fortune is ever seen accompanying industry.

—Oliver Goldsmith, author

Nobody who ever gave his best,
regretted it.

—George Halas, pro football coach

If you want to accomplish something, go do it!

—Rudyard Kipling, author

If people knew how hard I had to work to gain my mastery, it wouldn't seem wonderful at all.

—Michelangelo, sculptor, painter, architect and poet

Sweat is the cologne of accomplishment.

—Arthur Jones, writer

In my experience, there are no shortcuts, no easy solutions, no luck—not over the long haul.

—Y. A. Tittle, former NFL quarterback

Even if you're on the right track, you'll get run over if you just sit there.

—Will Rogers, humorist

Work hard at everything, every day. You don't go to a surgeon and have him say this was an off day for him.

—Alan King, entertainer

Half-finished work generally proves to be labor lost.

—Abraham Lincoln, former U.S. president

SIX

Be a Lifelong Learner

If you think your days of learning are over, think again.

Graduates often believe their learning years are behind them. But for those who want to maintain a sense of wonder, this should never be true. Evidence shows that keeping the brain engaged in the learning process is one secret to maintaining youth.

Take a look at these truths:

- People who read every day are less likely to suffer from Alzheimer's disease.
- Readers are alive and vibrant, sharp and alert—essential aspects to a youthful life.
- Learning keeps life interesting.

There are dozens of ways to keep learning into your adult years—even into your retirement years. You can learn about the Bible, you can take up a new hobby or craft, you can learn about gardening or history. You can take a course at your community college on cooking or foreign language.

The list is endless. What's important is that you keep your mind alive and active. A stale mind is an old mind, old before its time. Don't let that happen to you. Keep learning; keep reading.

The School of Churchill

How would Winston Churchill become a respected politician? The answer was obvious to Churchill. He would educate himself. He would use three or four hours in the middle of the day to read so he could learn everything in the field of politics.

As an intellectual exercise, Churchill wouldn't read the important debates until he'd first read the bill in question and mastered its implications. That way, he would record his own views on the bill, assessing the logic of his own opinions.

Churchill studied British institutional and political history, and ancient and modern philosophers, Plato, Aristotle, and Lecky. As if he were at a university, Churchill gave himself daily assignments, such as reading twenty-five pages of Gibbon, along with fifty pages of Macaulay.

One of the greatest compliments anyone ever gave Churchill was that he was his own university. Imagine what you could do if you created your own course load of topics that would help you in life, topics that would stimulate you to dream and keep your brain forever young.

The Chicken or the Egg?

Learning revolves around reading and writing. Or maybe it's writing and reading.

Writer Susan Sontag stated: "Reading usually precedes writing, and the impulse to write is almost always fired by reading something. Reading, the love of reading, is what makes you dream of becoming a writer."

The reason? Reading offers constant inspiration for the writer. It's the same way with any aspect of learning. Expose yourself to new things, new areas of knowledge you haven't mastered, and you will be inspired to master them.

It doesn't matter whether the inspiration or the learning comes first for you. Both are needed if you're going to live your life as a lifelong learner.

A Love Affair?

What are your thoughts about reading?

Many graduates leave school with a firm resolve that their reading days are behind them. "I hate reading," many of them will say. "I've spent enough time reading, now I'm going to step into the action."

The truth is, your "action" in life will be very limited if you don't spend time reading good books. Reading will offer knowledge and wisdom. Reading your Bible will give you greater insights into God's plan for your life. Reading novels will inspire you to new ways of seeing life, reading magazines will offer you practical tips about daily living. Reading books about history and current events will give you a good perspective on the past and the present.

Reading is the gateway to almost every new idea you'll ever experience.

Philosopher Silvestre de Sacy revealed his love affair with books when he said, "Oh, my darling books! A day will come when you will be laid out on the salesroom table, and others will buy and possess you . . . persons, perhaps, less worthy of you than your old master. Yet . . . how dear to me are they all! Have I not chosen them, one-by-one, gathered them in with the sweat of my brow? I do love you all!"

And you, graduate, would do well to feel the same way!

Coach's Corner

John Wooden, former men's basketball coach at UCLA, had eight laws of learning:

1. explanation	5. repetition
2. demonstration	6. repetition
3. imitation	7. repetition
4. repetition	8. repetition

Practice Makes Perfect

Learning is a terrific way to stay forever young. But learning involves more than exposing yourself to a dozen different new things. Learning requires that you take in information, dissect information, and analyze it. After that it requires that you use the knowledge you've picked up.

In other words, put it into practice.

Fred Rogers of *Mr. Roger's Neighborhood* fame, tells about the time when he was young and tried to learn everything all at once. In the same season he was being exposed to the piano, organ, algebra, cooking, typing and clarinet lessons. The problem was that he didn't practice.

"I think I wanted to learn by magic," Rogers says. "I had the idea that if I got the clarinet, I would know how to play it somehow. But magic doesn't work with learning. Not with anything really worthwhile."

Keep Swinging

Golfer Jack Nicklaus has always been a spokesman for learning. No matter how well he did on the pro tour, his emphasis was on learning, knowing more, and understanding the game in a deeper way than any of his peers.

"There may be a point in time when you don't get any better at golf, but that doesn't mean you ever stop learning," Nicklaus says. "Like it or not, life—like golf—is also about learning. Some people do stop learning and they are not being fair to themselves."

Nicklaus is right. In a life lived forever young, you must keep swinging, keep going after the ball, keep learning. Anything less is cheating yourself out of a much brighter future.

Satisfaction Guaranteed

Author Tim LaHaye likes to say, "If you wish to guarantee your child's unlimited vocational potential, help him to master the basics. Make sure he reads rapidly with strong emphasis on retention." Children are curious, by nature, and they will amaze you with the number of books they can read. Reading is the foundation of all learning. If a child can read well, he can learn almost anything. If he is a poor reader, he will find the educational process extremely difficult.

Keep learning now that school is over. Read often, and remember what you read. How? By talking about it. Just think . . . a way to keep your brain forever young, and find things to talk about on dates all at the same time!

Find a Friend

Statesman William Gladstone says books make a delightful society. If you go into a room and find it full of books . . . even without taking them from the shelves, they seem to speak to you . . . to bid you welcome. They seem to tell you they have something inside their covers that will be good for you, and that they are willing and desirous to impart it to you.

Books are a family of friends: friends for sale, lined up on the shelves of bookstores straight and proud waiting for you to pick them. In them you will find the material to expand your mind, soften your heart and stir your soul.

TV or Not TV?

Everywhere we look we hear about film stars. The latest television stars and movie moguls dominate the media and fill the covers of magazines lining the aisles of our Wal-Marts and supermarkets. With $10 billion spent in the film industry in 2004, you would think our country cared more about movies than anything else.

But that isn't the whole story.

What you don't hear is that each year Americans spend almost three times as much money—$25 billion—on books. In fact, the twenty-first century has been dubbed "The Age of the Book." More than 150,000 books are published each year, and online services such as Amazon.com carry up to three million titles at any given time.

Here's the true test, one that author Brian Tracy points out. Go into the home of a wealthy person and one of the first things you'll see is a well-stocked library. If you go into the home of poor people, what's the first thing you see? That's right—the biggest television they can afford.

The question to ponder: Did the owners of large homes become wealthy and then buy the books? Or did they buy the books, read them, and then become wealthy? It seems the answer is obvious. People buy books, study and apply them, and then find the types of careers that will give them wealth and significance.

Toss out the TV—or at least put it in the back room. And remember all the books you read through school? Consider them merely a foundation if you want to find your way to your own field of dreams!

Honest Educated Abe

Former president Abraham Lincoln had no formal education in his early years. But as he got older he set out on a quest for learning and self-improvement. He read incessantly—first the Bible, and then the works of Shakespeare. During his single term in the House of Representatives, his colleagues considered it humorous that Lincoln spent his spare time poring over books in the Library of Congress.

The result of this work of self-education was the intellectual power revealed in Lincoln's writing and speeches. Abe might've been as honest as the day is long, but if he hadn't taught himself how to read and write and reason, he never would've had the ability to write documents that made history.

Imagine the United States without the Emancipation Proclamation or the Gettysburg Address!

Be like Abe! Honest and educated!

Take It from a Master

Learning may seem like a bore to you today. After all, you just finished an arduous run of years in school, sitting in a classroom, taking in notes, studying for tests, gaining knowledge. But the learning process is part of why you're so excited today, part of why you can barely imagine how wonderful your future will be.

Some graduates leave school thinking it's time for a break, a hiatus from learning. Don't be one of those. This is the stage of life when learning gets fun because you are on your own and no one is looking over your shoulder and telling you what to do. Now—at the beginning of your adult years—you will be learning about the things that excite and thrill you, the things you dream about.

Consider Michelangelo. When he was thirteen years old he applied for an art apprenticeship in Florence, Italy. The man taking his application looked the boy up and down and sneered at him, "Can you draw?"

Michelangelo pulled himself up a little straighter and didn't blink. "I can learn."

Flash forward seventy-one years. Michelangelo, at age eighty-four, was asked to summarize his life's philosophy, the mind-set that made him such a master at the arts. Michelangelo did not hesitate. He said simply, "I still learn."

Say No to Flabby Brains

Your brain has to be used—much the way your arms and legs have to be used. Stop using your body and it'll turn flabby and useless. Stop using your brain, and the same thing happens.

Seminary Professor Howard G. Hendricks says an active brain is as important as a functioning body when it comes to battling the effects of aging. As long as you live you must learn, Hendricks says, and as long as you learn you will live life to the fullest.

Like a muscle, the mind develops with usage. It atrophies when not used.

Learning rejuvenates your brain, like getting together with a trainer at your local gym stimulates your body. You'll see results almost immediately, and even though there is some effort involved, you'll feel better, younger and more alive.

Whoa, There . . .

Learning is a wonderful way to stay young, but there are limits. First, you'll never know absolutely everything about anything. Second, you must be careful to use your learning for the right purposes.

Author Charles Swindoll once said, "I do not care what authority you have, how long you've studied in the field, how many advanced degrees you have earned, you are not the final word. You are still a learner, and God has the final word. I have found that the scholars who have taught me the most are the most teachable. We are all on a learning curve. I've learned some things from every intern I've mentored. Hopefully, they've picked up a few helpful things from me, as well."

Finally, learning can be destructive if the information you seek to obtain isn't good for you and your friends and family, even for society. Take, for example, the cruel dictators of the world. Many were learned men, but they used their knowledge for destruction.

Former president Ronald Reagan once said, "Learning is a good thing, but unless it is tempered by faith and a love of freedom, it can be very dangerous, indeed." The names of many intellectuals are recorded on the rolls of infamy, from Robespierre to Lenin to Ho Chi Minh to Pol Pot.

Pat's Perspective

You may have your degree in hand, but your education is just beginning. The world is changing so rapidly that all known knowledge is doubling every sixty-three days. To stay relevant in this game of life, we must be lifelong learners until our last breath.

The best way to be a lifelong learner is to be a lifelong reader. The problem is most young people don't read. In fact, the average man upon graduating from high school will not read another book the rest of his life. Women buy 85 percent of the books sold in this country.

If you will read an hour a day from books that you're interested in, at the end of one week you will have finished a book. At the end of one year, you will have finished fifty-two books, and at the end of ten years, you will have completed 520 books.

Do you realize how much knowledge and wisdom you will gain by reading 520 books over the next ten years? A staggering amount!!

Just about everything in my life depends on my reading. The speeches I give, the books that I write, the counseling I offer are all predicated on my reading. I am constantly reading from seven or eight books at a time and I try to complete one book every day.

Erasmus, the great educator, once said, "When I have money, I buy books. If I have anything left over, I buy food and clothes." That's the intensity and passion for reading all of us should have.

~

Books do not make life easier or more simple,
but harder and more interesting.

—Harry Golden, journalist and author

Learners will inherit the future.

—Eric Hoffer, philosopher

Learning often involves a certain amount of risk,
and one of the reasons mature people learn less than young
people is that they are less inclined to be risk-takers.

—John W. Gardner, author

Books are the quietest and most constant
of friends. They are the most accessible and wisest of
counselors and the most patient of teachers.

—Charles W. Eliot, educator

Learn as though you would never be able to master it;
hold it as though you would be in fear of losing it.

—Confucius, Chinese philosopher

They said that hitting was just something
that came naturally to me. I thought about baseball
constantly, and I made it a point to learn
what I could from older players.

—Henry "Hank" Aaron, baseball Hall of Fame member

*A field, however fertile, cannot be fruitful
without cultivation. Neither can the
mind, without learning.*

—Cicero, Roman statesman, orator and author

*The art and science of asking questions
is the source of all knowledge.*

—Dr. Adolf Berle, educator

Feedback is the breakfast of champions!

—Ken Blanchard, author

*Sparky Anderson tried to learn from every manager,
coach and player he came in contact with. He always
wanted to know what was going on, how things were
being done, and why they were being done.*

—Tommy Lasorda, former L.A. Dodgers coach

He who is afraid of asking, is afraid of learning.

—Dutch proverb

Ceading and learning
are indispensable to each other.

—John F. Kennedy, former U.S. president

I use not only all the brains I have,
but all I can borrow.

—Woodrow Wilson, former U.S. president

If you are not continually learning and
upgrading your skills, somewhere someone else is.
And when you meet that person, you will lose.

—Reid Buckley, speech coach

Cearning is a treasure that follows
its owner everywhere.

—Chinese proverb

Become addicted to constant and
never-ending self-improvement.

—Anthony J. D'Angelo, *The College Blue Book*

*Reading well is one of the great pleasures
that solitude can afford you.*

—Sir Francis Bacon,
British statesman and philosopher

*A book is a version of the world.
If you do not like it, ignore it . . . or offer
your own version in return.*

—Salman Rushdie, author

*Once you learn to read,
you will be forever free.*

—Frederick Douglass, civil rights leader

*When you sell someone a book,
you don't sell him just twelve ounces of paper
and ink and glue. You sell him
a whole new life.*

—Christopher Morley, actor

*A well-composed book is a magic carpet
on which we are wafted to a world that we
cannot enter in any other way.*

—Caroline Gordon, writer

*Reading is to the mind, what
exercise is to the body.*

—Sir Richard Steele, educator

*Regular readers are about
eight percent more likely to express
daily satisfaction.*

—Sir David Niven, actor

SEVEN

Laugh Long and Loud

Years from now, when you think back to your school days, you'll be tempted to smile and shake your head.

"Those were the good old days," you'll probably say. "We sure had a great time."

What was so good about the time you're just wrapping up? Why were the times so great? The answer is something that will help you stay forever young—your school days included a lot of laughter.

You sat with your friends and laughed through lunch, walked with your classmates and laughed in the hallways, and gathered at each other's houses to laugh about the things you laughed about. Don't miss the fact that laughing will keep you young.

Laughing Livers Live Longer

Proverbs 17:22 (NIV) says a cheerful heart is good medicine. For centuries people considered that a cliché, but as medical research kicked in, the words took on another meaning. Today there are volumes of research that back up the claim that laughter is good for us physically, emotionally and mentally.

The liver is the largest organ in the body, a filter needed for optimal health on all levels. Laughter is the only activity that gives our livers a workout. This discovery gives credence to this verse in Proverbs. Yes, a cheerful heart is good medicine.

Wise Words

Laughter is the best medicine anyone can get. It stirs up the blood, expands the chest, electrifies the nerves, clears away the cobwebs from the brain, and rehabilitates your whole body. Take a look at what these people say about humor:

Author and speaker Barbara Johnson encourages others by saying, "Develop a sense of humor to carry you through the days. Without one you are doomed to despair. With one, you can survive and actually enjoy the trip."

Bill Gates credited his success to the fact that he works because it's fun. "I guess you could say that I approach business as a kind of problem-solving challenge," Gates said. "That doesn't mean I don't take business seriously, because I do, but life is a lot more fun, if you treat its challenges in creative ways."

Author and pastor Chuck Swindoll believes that people who consistently laugh do so in spite of the trouble they face.

"They pursue fun, rather than wait for it to knock on their door, in the middle of the day," Swindoll said. "Such infectiously joyful believers have no trouble convincing people around them that Christianity is real and that Christ can transform a life. Joy is the flag that flies above the castle of their hearts, announcing that the King is in residence!"

Let your flag fly high!

Funeral for a Fish

Can you find humor in the sad times?

Certainly.

Patti Reagan tells the story about her father, the late president Ronald Reagan: "When I was about eight, I had a black fish named Blackie. One day Blackie was lying in the bottom of the tank. At first I insisted he was asleep, but once he floated to the top, my father said, 'Well, he's dead.'

"To make the impact a little lighter on me, he gave Blackie a fish funeral. We went out back and my father dug a little grave for Blackie. He tied two sticks together with string, to make a cross, and he delivered a eulogy for the fish. I was so into this ceremony, and I was having so much fun, that when it ended, and after my father asked me if I felt better, I said, 'Yeah, can we go kill another one?'"

What had been a sad moment in Patti Reagan's childhood remains a memory that gives her a smile. Why? Because her father understood the importance of humor. Try to live your life the same way.

Sports Special

The most important thing you will ever understand about sports is that it has to be fun. If the journey to the state title isn't a fun one, then that glorious moment won't matter at all.

"The medals don't mean anything, and the glory doesn't last," said track star Jackie Joyner-Kersee. "It's all about your happiness. The rewards are going to come, but my happiness is just loving the sport and having fun, performing."

Practicing sports has to be fun. Look for ways to connect with teammates, and remind yourself often that you're doing that hard work because you like it. Carol Heiss, the 1960 Olympic gold medal women's figure-skating winner, loved talking about how fun her practicing hours were.

"My mother was marvelous. She made going to practice fun!" Heiss said. "I remember one Christmas Eve, I was looking forward to a day off from practicing. Then Mom said, 'Carol, won't it be great tomorrow, on Christmas Day? You'll have the ice all to yourself. You can train for five hours and no one will be there but us!'"

Life will be full of practice hours, whether you're playing a sport or working on a business project. The key to living life forever young is to enjoy the journey. When you do, the victory will be sweeter than you ever dreamed.

Find the Funniness

Right now the idea of working to find the funny moments in life is, well, funny. Laughter comes often and easily for you. But as you move into the working world with time clocks and grouchy bosses, deadlines and high expectations, laughter is a little harder to come by.

That's why you need to look for the funny, lighthearted moments. Karen Kingsbury, the number one bestselling CBA novelist who helped write this book, tells a story of being several years into her career writing emotional adult fiction.

"Most of my work was so deep, so emotional," Karen says, "the only way to get through it was if some of the scenes were funny."

Karen didn't only look for things to laugh about, she prayed that she'd find them.

"I asked God to show me something so funny I'd have to include it in a book," Karen recalls. "Then I looked harder than ever."

Karen began to see her everyday interactions with her children, her husband, her editors and her agent as being more laughable than before. Everything about her daily routine felt lighter, and she laughed far more than usual.

Her husband even commented that she looked younger.

"He thought I was using some new expensive face cream," Karen says. "At the time I didn't make the connection, but after a week or so I figured it out. I wasn't younger. I had no new facial cure. I simply was taking time to laugh, the way I did back in my school days."

Later that month, Karen visited Marine World with her family. As they rushed to the sea lion show, Karen's children wanted ice cream. Glancing at her watch, Karen looked at her husband and shrugged. "Sure," he told her. "Let's get the kids an ice cream cone."

The worker at the snack shack was robotically slow and apparently hadn't received much training in the art of filling a cone. He would swirl the ice cream around and around the perimeter of the cone, and then as it neared seven inches high the ice cream would topple over onto the floor. He was three for five before the job was done.

Meanwhile, the music was starting in the nearby Sea Lion Stadium. Karen grabbed her son's hand and set off running—her husband and other kids close behind. A few steps out, the ice cream atop one of the cones in Karen's hand flopped off the cone and straight into Karen's shoe. Undaunted, she grabbed a stack of napkins and a replacement scoop of ice cream (in a bowl). Then she and her family raced to the top of the Sea Lion Stadium.

The place was packed. Karen spotted a single open row about two-thirds of the way down. "There," she pointed. "Let's hurry."

By now, the sea lions were on the stage and everyone was intently watching the opening of the show. Karen set off down the stairs, but there was a problem. The stairs varied in size, standard stair, mini-stair, standard stair, mini-stair. Stadiums sometimes use this type of stairway to save space, making the steps steeper. But Karen didn't realize this until it was too late.

On the second step, she tripped and fell to the ground and because of the steepness of the incline, began to tumble down the stairs and into the stadium. From the corner of her eye she noticed some of the patrons swinging their video cameras toward her, gawking in surprise. Three people started clapping.

At the same time, the sea lions—in unison—swung their heads in her direction. She had not only stopped the show, she had become part of it. Items began falling from her backpack. Karen had been in charge of the family's sweatshirts, water bottles, apples and souvenirs. Now, because the backpack wasn't zipped all the way shut, an occasional apple or water bottle would crash loose from the bag and bounce quickly to the bottom of the stadium.

Finally people realized Karen wasn't part of the act. They started sticking out feet and arms in desperate attempts to break her fall. When she finally stopped tumbling and stood up, she was surprised to see that she was standing right next to the empty row—the one where she'd wanted her family to sit.

"At that point, my legs could've both been broken and still I wasn't going to let people know I was in pain." Karen laughed. "I waved everyone off, letting them believe I was okay. Then I sat down and motioned for my husband and kids to join me."

Two of her children ran to the bottom of the stadium to collect apples, water bottles, and a random comb that had fallen from her backpack. Then her family gathered around her and watched the show. Not until it was over did she turn back to her husband and say, without cracking a smile, "Okay. So how did that look?"

Until then, her husband hadn't let loose a trace of laughter, but then he began laughing with tears streaming down his face. The laughter continued throughout the day and to this day, still. When Karen arrived home that night, she realized God had answered her prayer. He had given her something hysterically funny, something she could include in one of her books. The story you just read is written in detail in her novel, *A Time to Dance,* as if it had happened to the character, Abby Reynolds.

By the way, Karen didn't hurt anything in the fall. Just her pride.

One of the best ways to approach work is to laugh along the way. Now, as you leave the graduation stage, make a point of taking your job seriously enough to glorify God, and lightly enough to laugh a lot.

Marge's Magic

At one of the major international airports in the Pacific Northwest, a woman in her late fifties has found a way to laugh in her job as security checkpoint officer. Marge Browning's job is to keep the line moving as people head to their gates.

Many people in her job would spend the eight-hour shift shouting, "Move along!" or "Have your laptop computers out of your bags!" or "Take off all jackets and jewelry!" Not Marge. She spends the time teasing people in line. "Sir, if you don't move ahead I'll buy you the double espresso myself."

Or "Come on folks, get friendly. It's six o'clock in the morning—what better time to be friendly." By the time people get through Marge's line, everyone's laughing, sleepy-eyed travelers, grumpy business folks, and other security personnel.

Most of all, Marge is laughing.

I spoke at a corporate event in Burlington, Vermont, the city where Ben and Jerry first made their ice cream. It's now an international success story. Why? Because ice cream is about fun and laughter, and Ben and Jerry have made their product fun . . . from the jazzy artwork on the cartons to the funny names of the ice cream itself—Funky Monkey, Cherry Garcia, etc. The entire experience is a blast. Not the picture you graduates usually get when you think about work.

Oval Office Humor

In September 1862, President Abraham Lincoln had just finished writing an important document when he called a special session of his closest advisors. When they arrived, he was reading a book by a well-known humorist. He read some of the book out loud.

At the end he laughed heartily, but his advisors sat, unsmiling, disapproving of the president's laughter. Lincoln said, "Why don't you laugh? With the fearful strain that is upon me night and day, if I did not laugh I should die, and you need this medicine as much as I do." The document he'd been writing? The Emancipation Proclamation.

Robert Farrell, founder of Farrell's Ice Cream Parlors, liked to say he didn't sell ice cream, he sold a good time. Ice cream was merely the vehicle. In the process, he built Farrell's into a wildly successful chain where families could gather for nonalcoholic, safe, good fun.

What was his secret to success? Atmosphere. The way laughter makes a room lighter, so Farrell made his ice cream parlors places of light. Everything from the red-flocked wallpaper to the singing waiters made for a fun and funny atmosphere. The fun of Farrell's brought people back again and again—the same way a laugh will in your relationships.

The Easter Bunny Flies Southwest

Herb Kelleher, former head of Southwest Airlines, runs the most consistently successful and profitable airline in the United States. Kelleher has a sense of humor that is contagious and infiltrates the entire company. He is known as the most outrageous CEO in the country, and he runs his company with people skills that involve laughter among other things.

Some examples? Kelleher has appeared at corporate headquarters dressed as Elvis and once—on one of his flights—as the Easter bunny. His attitude, of course, carries down the chain of command all the way to the newest employees. Ever been on a Southwest flight? You'll find flight attendants who often seem like stand-up comics. The outcome? Southwest Airlines continues to grow larger every year. One of the reasons? Herb Kelleher's ability to laugh!

Pat's Perspective

I have a very good friend named Ken Hussar who lives in Lancaster, Pennsylvania. For almost thirty years, we have been collecting one-line humor to use in our speaking careers and share with other people.

Ken and I both agree that there is no sweeter sound than a room of people howling in laughter over some well-placed jokes that tickle their funny bones.

One of Walt Disney's cardinal rules of life was to have fun.

Thomas Edison said, "I never worked a day in my life. It was all fun!" When President Theodore Roosevelt was in the White House raising a brood of rambunctious teenage boys, whenever they would leave his office, he would yell at them, "Have all the fun you can!!"

Obviously, there are serious moments in life, but I have discovered if you are having fun in work, in play and at home, everything runs a lot more smoothly. And the people around you are enjoying their lives a lot more as well.

Starting today, I hereby authorize you to have all the fun you can the rest of your life! You can thank me later for that little piece of wisdom.

~

*It is a mark of intelligence, no matter what you
are doing, to have a good time doing it.*

—Ruth Benedict, anthropologist

*I smile because I'm so happy. This isn't a job for me;
it's fun. Everything about the game is fun.*

—Dwight Howard, Orlando Magic rookie, age nineteen

*A person can survive without food
and drink over a long period of time, but
no man can live long without humor.*

—Joseph P. Lennon, author

I have seen what a laugh can do.
It can transform almost unbearable tears
into something bearable—
even hopeful.

—Bob Hope, entertainer

Laughter is to life, what shock absorbers
are to automobiles. It won't take the potholes out of
the road, but it sure makes the ride smoother.

—Barbara Johnson, speaker/writer

If it isn't fun, why do it?

—Jerry Greenfield,
cofounder of Ben & Jerry's.

We smile because we want to,
not because we have to.

—Herb Kelleher,
former CEO of Southwest Airlines

I realize that humor isn't for everyone.
It's only for people who want to have fun,
enjoy life and feel alive.

—Anne Wilson Schaef, writer

I'm not happy; I'm cheerful.
There's a difference.
A happy woman has no cares at all.
A cheerful woman has cares but has
learned how to deal with them.

—Beverly Sills, singer

The simple truth is that happy people
generally don't get sick.

—Bernie S. Siegel, M.D., writer

EIGHT

Choose to Dance

There are two ways to approach life—sit it out or dance.

The sitters will age quickly, no longer excited about the coming day or year, no longer taken with dreams and passions and goals, no longer grateful for the gifts they possess or the people they love.

But the dancers . . . these are the ones who will hold on to their youth, because they will hold on to their excitement and enthusiasm. The dance of life is the art of seizing the day, embracing the moment, and squeezing every bit of life out of every single breath.

Life must be lived with passion, energy and enthusiasm, not just in the early years, but until your last breath is drawn. If you want to be forever young, if you want to hold on to the excitement of today, you need to live intentionally, with purpose, having a plan and a dream bigger than yourself.

To dance is to have enthusiasm for life. Enthusiasm means to be filled with God's divine spirit. It comes from the Greek words "en" (in) and "theos" (God). Enthusiastic people possess a dynamism and an inner drive that seems divinely inspired.

Here's the key: Every man is enthusiastic at times. One man has enthusiasm for thirty minutes, another for thirty days. But as scientist Edward B. Butler said, "It is the man who has it for thirty years who makes a success of his life."

Past, Future and Present

Life includes three blocks of time: The past, the future and the present. The past is a valuable learning tool, but it should be a springboard, not a hammock. Too often we get bogged down in the mire of the past. You must learn from your past mistakes, but not lean on your past successes. While the future is exciting and limitless, it has not arrived yet.

We must pour out all our energy into the present. Max out today by sucking the marrow from the bones of the moment. Drain the cup dry today and you will automatically invest in tomorrow. And tomorrow is worth investing in. The trouble is, too many people wait until tomorrow to think about tomorrow. Or they spend today dreaming about tomorrow, without getting any real benefit out of the moment.

All that can be changed. You must find clear-cut definite goals for every stage of life. Goals should be relied on, reviewed often, and revised when necessary. Hard work is a part of making these goals a reality, and it's in the hard work, the going after life that you will find yourself dancing. Albert Einstein said, "If you want to live a happy life, tie it to a goal—not to people or things."

Just Say No for Success

Sometimes the word "no" gets a bad rap. The very meaning of the word is negative, but sometimes a number of no's add up to a very wonderful yes. Here are some examples:

- Say no to junk food, and you'll be saying yes to the joys of healthy living.
- Say no to drugs, and you'll be saying yes to a clean mind and a life free of addiction.
- Say no to laziness, and you'll be saying yes to a life of hard work and success.

A sixteen-year-old Boston student, Susan Cho, performed a beautiful masterpiece at her piano solo in the city's arts auditorium. A number of college music professors were in attendance, and when her performance was finished, Susan was approached by many of them. Each had information about their university, and several made scholarship offers to the brilliant pianist.

The opportunity gave Susan a great chance to say yes. But only after a lifetime of Susan previously saying "no." No to thousands of hours of TV, dozens of invitations to see a movie, and hundreds of other activities. Susan would say no so that she could stay home and practice the piano.

But in the end, her yes was worth more than all the no's combined.

Work the Steps

Hard work makes dreams come true, no doubt about that, but hard work doesn't come without self-discipline. Pastor John MacArthur gives seven steps to learning self-discipline.

1. Start small. Begin with your room. Clean it, then keep it clean. When something is out of place, train yourself to put it where it belongs. Then extend that discipline of neatness to the rest of your house.

2. Be on time. That may not sound very spiritual or profound, but it's important. If you're supposed to be somewhere at a specific time, be there on time! Develop the ability to discipline your desires, activities and schedules so that you can arrive on time.

3. Do the hardest job first. That will prevent the hardest jobs from being left undone.

4. Organize your life. Plan the use of your time; don't just react to circumstances. Use a calendar and make a daily list of things you need to accomplish. If you don't control your time, everything else will.

5. Accept correction. Correction helps make you more disciplined because it shows you what you need to avoid. Don't avoid criticism, accept it gladly.

6. Practice self-denial. Learn to say no to your feelings. Occasionally deny yourself things that are all right just for the purpose of mastering yourself. Learn to do what you know to be right

even if you don't feel like it. Cultivating discipline in the physical realm will help us become disciplined in our spiritual lives.

7. Welcome responsibility. When you have an opportunity to do something that needs to be done, volunteer for it if you have a talent in that area. Welcoming responsibility forces you to get yourself organized.

Your Greatest Resource

Author Peter Drucker wrote: "Time is the one truly universal condition. All work takes place in time and uses up time. Yet most people take for granted this unique, irreplaceable, and necessary resource."

It's true. Think of some of your other resources—money, health and intellect. Money can be lost and gained over time, health can be restored by a change of habits, and intellect can be improved through study and lifelong learning.

But time is altogether different.

Every second that passes is a second you can never get back. You may not fully understand that until you've had some more birthdays, but treat time like your greatest resource, and you'll get the most out of every day.

Wise Old Abe

In an address to the Wisconsin State Agricultural Society on September 30, 1859, Abraham Lincoln told of an Eastern monarch who asked his counselors to formulate a truth that would apply to all times and situations. After careful consideration, they returned with this sentence: "And this too shall pass away."

Lincoln loved that saying.

He thought those words said much about both the blessings and burdens of life. If the blessings will pass, then a person has no room for pride. If the burdens will pass, then a person has no room for lingering pain.

"In both my happiest and saddest moments," Lincoln said, "I remember to tell myself, 'This too shall pass.' Those words have not only quieted my heart in times of trial, but they have also aroused me from my lethargy. They have made me realize the importance of using wisely the fleeting days God has allotted to me."

Lincoln was right. Treat each day as a gift.

Wait a Second

Find a clock or stopwatch with a second hand. Sit down, stare at that second hand and watch it move through sixty seconds. One minute. Those seconds are the way we measure time, but more than that, they are the very essence of our lives. What we will do with our lives comes down to how we spend our seconds. Those precious tick . . . tick . . . ticks on the clock.

If you live seventy-five years, you will live approximately 2.5 billion seconds. Make up your mind now to use every one of those in a way that will send you to bed with a smile.

Bernard Berenson, an internationally renowned art critic, had a zest for life. Even when he was in poor health, he cherished every moment.

Shortly before he died, at age ninety-four, he said to a friend, "I would willingly stand on the street corner, hat in hand, asking passersby to drop their unused minutes into it."

Keep that in mind the next time you're looking to kill an hour.

Moments in a Life

If you're going to dance through this life, start today. Sometimes it helps to break down the moments in a day, the moments in a lifetime, in order to see just exactly what most people have at their disposal.

Teacher Richard W. DeHaan explains it this way:

If you live sixty-five years, you have about 600,000 hours. If you're eighteen when you completed high school, you'll have forty-seven years, or 412,000 hours to live after graduation.

If you spend eight hours a day sleeping, eight hours for personal, social and recreational activities, and eight hours for working, that breaks down to about 137,333 hours in each category. Just 137,333 hours to accomplish your career goals. Only 137,333 hours for family time and memory-making.

Doesn't seem like much, does it? In the light of eternity, it's but a fleeting moment. How important, then, that we spend our waking hours wisely.

Count It for Christ

D. J. DePree, a former member of the Radio Bible Class board of directors who lived to be almost one hundred years old, calculated his age in terms of days. Someone would ask D. J. how old he was, and immediately he would answer with the number of days. He came up with the idea after spending time studying Psalm 90:12, which tells us to number our days so that we'll gain a heart of wisdom.

DePree took this literally. In the process he was reminded of the swift passage of time, and the reason for living life with eternity in view. Days, he believed, were tools to help him grow closer to God, tools to help him tell others about the saving grace of Jesus Christ.

Today is here and gone—and it'll be that way with your life, too. Sure, right now your future seems to stretch out endlessly. It's like that for all graduates, but soon you'll be looking back wondering where your life went. Make a decision right now not only to spend your day with zest and zeal, not only to dance and seize the day, but to seize it for Christ.

That way, when you take time to count the days, you'll be sure to make them count for Christ!

Pat's Perspective

I am asked all the time, "How do you get everything done in your life? Are your days longer than twenty-four hours? Do you ever sleep at night?" No, my days are no longer than yours and I need a good night's sleep as much as you do.

I do have a couple of secrets, though, about maximizing every minute of the day.

My wife, Ruth, teaches time management and organizational skills, so that's a wonderful advantage in my life. Here in three simple steps are Ruth's words of wisdom about living each day to the fullest:

First, start each day full of zest. Goldie Hawn was once asked her secret of success. She answered, "Want to know my secret of success? I love life. I wake up every morning just excited to get up!" Why would Goldie Hawn be so excited to get up? She spends time on things that are important to her.

So, second, make sure you know what is really important to you. Right now, what would you say are the five most important things and people in your life? What are you most passionate about? What do you value most? Write them down. Reflect on how you want to live them and then make it happen. If you spend every day focusing on the things that matter most to you, you will be excited to get up also.

And, finally, to make sure you do spend time on these things, you must plan them. Before your week begins, take ten to fifteen minutes planning to spend time on the most important things and people in your life. Actually write them into your schedule throughout the week. And then as you progress through your week, you see those things in writing and remember to do them. Therefore, writing them down is a must. Otherwise, smaller insignificant things get in the way and we "forget."

The tendency of most people is to focus on what's "in your face." The key is to focus on what's important. When you are doing that on a consistent basis, you will live life with zest!

Today is a piece of your life that will
never come again. Use or lose it!

—Abraham Lincoln, former U.S. president

It's not the heavy minutes that eventually wear
a man down, but the wasted ones.

—Phil Taylor, writer

Do you love life? Then don't waste time,
for that is the stuff life is made of.

—Benjamin Franklin, statesman and philosopher

As a well-spent day brings happy sleep,
so life well-used brings happy death.

—Leonardo da Vinci, painter

Write on your heart that each day is
the best day of the year.

—Ralph Waldo Emerson, essayist and poet

*Like a bridge, man was designed to
carry the load of the moment; not the combined
weight of a year all at once.*

—William Ward, poet and author

*Until you value yourself, you won't value your time.
Until you value your time, you will
not do anything with it.*

—M. Scott Peck, author

*You are younger today than you will ever be again.
Make use of it, for the sake of tomorrow.*

—Anonymous

*All of us tend to put off living.
We are all dreaming of some magical rose garden,
over the horizon, instead of enjoying the roses that
are blooming outside our windows today.*

—Dale Carnegie, author

Do today's duty; fight today's temptations.
Do not weaken and distract yourself, by looking
forward to things you cannot see and could
not understand if you saw them.

—Charles Kingsley, writer

Every day is a 3–2 pitch or a foul shot
to win the game. You've got to toe the line
and produce, every day.

—Glenn Harris, sportscaster

Ordinary people merely think how they shall spend
their time; a man of talent tries to use it.

—Arthur Schopenhauer, philosopher

Being a professional is doing the things
you love to do on the days when you
don't feel like doing them.

—Julius Erving, former NBA star

I beg you, cherish the day, live it, enjoy it, savor it!

—Mary Higgins Clark, author

Live every day like it's your last.
Someday, you'll be right.

—Preacher Roe, former baseball pitcher

Old or young, we're on our last cruise.
Make it mean something.

—Robert Louis Stevenson, author

Ask yourself this question:
Will this matter a year from now?

—Richard Carlson, author

You have to count on living every single day,
in a way you believe will make you feel good about
your life so that if it were over tomorrow,
you'd be content with yourself.

—Jane Seymour, actress

No matter what your goals in life,
the best way to prepare for tomorrow is
to do what you can today.

—Charles Percy, former U.S. senator

NINE

Handle the Hard Times

Loss is a part of life.

The person who grows old and hard is one who is afraid to grieve, afraid to cry, one who is unable or unwilling to handle the hard times. But you—on your quest to live life forever young— will need to understand that hard times happen to everyone. You must do your best to embrace them.

Never be caught by surprise when hard times happen. Yes, they will be difficult, and yes, they will lead us through a valley we never expected to walk through. But it is through the tough times of life that we have the opportunity to grow and mature.

One stumbling block to handling the hard times is having an unrealistic view of them. When hard times come, there is a temptation to give up on God or life. God gave us a plan about how to handle hard times when they come.

Jesus promised us we'd have hard times. At the end of a long talk with his friends, Jesus summed up his thoughts in John 16:33 (NIV) by saying: "I have told you these things, so that in me you may have peace. In this world you will have trouble. But take heart! I have overcome the world."

In this world you will have trouble. It's a fact of life. The difference between those who will lose their zest for life and those who live life young at heart is their ability to understand and handle that trouble.

A Trip Through the Valley

The twenty-third Psalm is often read at funeral services. Why? Because it talks about God's presence, about his ability to be with us and to lead us by still waters, to quiet and restore our souls.

But the Psalm doesn't stop there. Take a look at the following verse from Psalm 23:4 (NIV): "Even though I walk through the valley of the shadow of death, I will fear no evil, for you are with me; your rod and your staff they comfort me."

Did you catch it?

Jesus doesn't tell us he'll walk with us around the valley of the shadow of death. He says he'll walk with us through the valley. The shadow of death is that dark place where morning seems to never come again, the cold, drafty place where death appears to have the last word.

It is there, in your darkest hour, that Jesus promises to be with us as we walk to the other side. The valley of the shadow of death is not a permanent place. It is a journey, a short trip. But it is only a short trip if you allow God to lead you, and if you believe his promises that morning will eventually come again.

Cry a Tear for Me

There are two little words in the Bible that give us a unique picture of how Jesus handled hard times. Jesus had been making the rounds in neighboring villages when he received word that his good friend Lazarus was sick.

By the time Jesus arrived at the house where Lazarus and his two sisters lived, Lazarus was dead and the entire household was grieving and wailing. Amidst accusations and criticisms for not showing up sooner, Jesus faced the family and friends of Lazurus and said, "Where have you laid him?"

They asked Jesus to follow them, and when they arrived at the grave site, Jesus wept (John 11:35, NIV). A few minutes later, Jesus would raise his friend from the dead.

But in the moment of sorrow, Jesus knew what to do.

We'd be much more likely to hold on to our young hearts if we would do the same. Yes, Jesus was a tough guy. He was the one who turned over the tables in the temples, so he was strong, too. But he wept because he came to earth to be an example to all of us of how to live. And when hard times hit him right in the face, Jesus allowed his emotions to acknowledge the pain. He registered the loss.

And he wept.

Another Cup of Lemonade, Please

You have two choices when hard times hit. You can give up or you can offer your hard times to God and let him use them to make you stronger, better, wiser. Or you can give up. Those are your only choices.

Robert L. Ripley was just beginning a career as a professional baseball player when he fell awkwardly on his pitching arm. The results were devastating: a fracture that would sideline him for the rest of the season.

Someone has probably told you that when life gives you lemons, make lemonade. That's just what Ripley did. To pass the time he taught himself to draw, which led to a job as a newspaper sports cartoonist. Soon he developed his famous *Ripley's Believe It or Not!* feature, a cartoon strip people are still talking about today.

That's the way you stay forever young. When your present dream is sidelined, look for something better. In addition, you might just acquire a taste for lemonade!

The Power of One

Now that you've made it this far, you've no doubt had to make some difficult choices. During your school years, hard times might have been your decision to say no to drinking or drugs, maybe your decision to say no to something illegal or immoral. Or maybe your hard times involved something you said yes to and later regretted.

Either way, you know what's right. You know and deep within your heart want to seek the good and godly, the right path.

It's been said that all living things are forced to become strong through resistance. The tougher the challenge, the greater the strength that results.

Take a drive sometime and notice the trees. Ever wonder why the strongest, biggest, most sturdy trees are the trees that stand alone in open fields? Think about it. The lone tree faces weather and wind and every aspect of the elements without the shielding of other trees. It is strong because it has no other choice. Hard times have made it strong.

That's how it is when we choose to stand up for what's right, when people we counted as friends turn against us because of our stance. There is power in one. And the good news is this—you never really stand alone.

God is with you and he always will be.

The Price of the Pearl

As you set out upon the journey of life, be aware that hard times will happen. The most successful people are those who have overcome adversity. People who have handled the heartache of loss or defeat or failure or illness or death, always come out on the other side stronger for the experience.

Educator Booker T. Washington once said, "Success isn't measured by the position you reach in life; it's measured by the obstacles you overcome."

Consider the oyster. One day, a small grain of sand— hardly worth noticing—slips between the oyster's shells. At first it's only a small irritant, really. Nothing too serious. But eventually that grain of sand causes the oyster great discomfort so that it becomes an all-encompassing problem, a major irritant.

What does the oyster do?

This perfect, brainless life form—designed by God—begins to wrap secretions called mother-of-pearl around the irritation, allowing the area to heal. Over time, the grain actually becomes bigger, and one day, when the oyster is harvested, there is proof that God was there all along, because the grain of sand has become a pearl, a priceless gem. And those oysters that are never wounded are fit only for an oyster stew.

That's Goofy

Once there was a young man just out of school who dreamed of working at a major magazine. For two years he did his best to get an interview with the magazine's editor, and for two years nothing was available.

That's when his big break came.

A position opened up as a copy boy, and the secretary at the magazine scheduled him for an interview. This was going to be the biggest break of his career. If he could get hired as an artist for the magazine, he'd have it made. He'd work awhile as a copy boy, and then move up to an assistant position.

One day he might even run the magazine's art department. That was the young man's deepest desire.

Finally the day of the interview arrived. The young man dressed his best, and with trembling knees he made his way to the office of the editor. Once the interview was underway, the editor spent some time with the boy, looking at his clip file of drawings and articles.

After five long minutes, the editor looked up and frowned. "You're no good, son." He slid the young man's file across the table back to him. "We're looking for someone else."

"No good?" The young man was crushed. He'd waited two years for this interview. For two years he dreamed about the position and the climb he'd make once he got hired. "How am I no good?"

"Well," the editor gestured toward the young man's file. "You're not creative."

"I'm not?" The young man couldn't believe what he was hearing. He stood, tucking his file under his arm. "Are you sure?"

"Son, listen to me," the man said. "You don't have a creative bone in your body."

When the young man got home, he was struck by the disappointment. Without question it was his darkest hour. But even as he sat there he began to handle it. He straightened himself up and made a plan.

If the magazine didn't want him, he'd do his artwork on his own. Maybe someday someone would buy his work, and then the magazine would be sorry. In the end, that's just what happened.

The young man's name?

Walt Disney.

God's the Coach

As far as NFL quarterback Trent Dilfer is concerned, every game he plays is ultimately coached by God.

"I've made some huge mistakes, but God has orchestrated them perfectly, and used every single one to mold me as a person," Dilfer has said. "Through molding me as a person, He's going to mold me into a better football player, too."

The same goes for you. God will take all the events in your life, good and bad, and use them to shape and mold you into exactly the person he wants you to be.

Pat's Perspective

A few years ago I wrote my autobiography, *Ahead of the Game*. I was fifty-nine years old at the time so I had a lot of ground to cover in this book. I shared my story as openly as possible, which included all of my successful ventures like graduating from college, starting my career in sports, winning an NBA championship in Philadelphia in 1983, and helping to start the Orlando Magic as an expansion team in the late eighties. Those were wonderful moments that I still enjoy thinking about today.

However, I also shared in the book my tough times, my failures and my heartaches. And, believe me, there were plenty of them. As I finished writing the book, this thought hit me hard—it was through the tough times, the losses and setbacks, that I did my greatest amount of growing and maturing. The good times were really fun, but I don't know how much I learned.

Through the tough times, I learned a lot. You don't have to go out and seek problems and difficult circumstances. They will come to you in the flow of life. Back in the early seventies when I was the general manager of the Chicago Bulls, I was going through some very difficult situations in my job. I arranged a meeting with my pastor, Dr. Warren Wiersbe. As I shared my struggles with him, Dr. Wiersbe simply said, "Now, Pat, don't waste your sufferings." That's not what I wanted to hear from him, but as I look back, it was some of the best advice I've ever received.

Keep learning and growing through your tough times and you'll be able to say with me, "Dr. Wiersbe, thanks for the good advice."

~

A smooth sea never made a skilled mariner.

—English Proverb

Make the best of your circumstances.
No one has everything, and everyone has some sorrow
mixed in with the gladness of life. The trick is to
make the laughter out-weigh the tears.

—Robert Louis Stevenson, author

Obstacles cannot crush me.
Every obstacle yields to stern resolve.

—Leonardo da Vinci, painter

In one of our concert grand pianos,
243 taut strings exert a pull of 40,000 pounds
on an iron frame. It is proof that out of great
tension may come great harmony.

—Theodore E. Steinway,
president of Steinway and Sons

Between grief and nothing,
I will take grief.

—William Faulkner, author

No experience is a bad experience unless
you learn nothing from it.

—Lyndon Baines Johnson,
former U.S. president

The Chinese word for "crisis" is the same
as that for "opportunity."

—Anonymous

I thank God for my handicaps,
for through them I have found myself,
my work, and my God.

—Helen Keller, lecturer

Birds sing after a storm. Why shouldn't we?

—Rose Fitzgerald Kennedy,
mother of former U.S. president John F. Kennedy

He who has never failed somewhere,
that man cannot be great.

—Herman Melville, author

There are defeats
more triumphant than victories.

—Author unknown

Most people are nicer after they've had
their heart broken a couple of times.

—Emma Thompson, actor

*I refuse to allow a disability to
determine how I live my life.*

—Christopher Reeve, actor

*You show me a sailboat in a calm sea,
and I'll show you a ship that
doesn't get anywhere.*

—George Steinbrenner,
owner, New York Yankees

*Every life has experienced pain and
failure at some time. The ones who have succeeded
are the ones who could put failure behind them and
move onward with a new dream, a new hope.*

—Anonymous

*Trouble is a part of life, and if you don't share it,
you don't give others the chance
to love you enough.*

—Dinah Shore, entertainer

Character cannot be developed in ease and quiet.
Only through experience of trial and suffering
can the soul be strengthened.

—Helen Keller, lecturer

On those days when you feel the worst,
when you think that everything is hopeless;
sometimes the best things happen.

—Walker Percy, author

Tragedy offers you a different perspective on life.
There are far more important things
than wins and losses.

—Tommy John, former major league pitcher

The ultimate measure of a man is not
where he stands in moments of comfort and
convenience, but where he stands at times
of challenge and controversy.

—Anonymous

TEN

Love Easily and Often

The final way to stay forever young is to love. Love like there's no tomorrow, love easily and without expectations of a response from others. Love and you will be doing what God created you to do. When we love we are nourishing our spirit and honoring God at the same time.

Jesus sums up love in 1 Corinthians 13:4–8,13 (NIV) with the following words:

> *Love is patient, love is kind. It does not envy, it does not boast, it is not proud. It is not rude, it is not self-seeking, it is not easily angered, it keeps no record of wrongs. Love does not delight in evil but rejoices with the truth. It always protects, always trusts, always hopes, always perseveres.*
>
> *Love never fails. . . .*
>
> *And now these three remain: faith, hope and love. But the greatest of these is love.*

If you want a life that's forever young you'd do well to make each of these a part of your life:

- Love for God—This will always be the building block for every other kind of love. Your dependence upon, gratitude for, and longing toward your Creator is a love that defies boundaries.
- Friendship love—This is love that you demonstrate by caring, spending time with someone whose heart is closely connected to yours. You are always looking out for the needs of someone special in your life.
- Relational love—This is love that is marked by a strong connection and emotional attachment to a family member (mother, father, brother, sister, etc). This love involves making time for that person, as well as acts of service and kindness on their behalf.
- Romantic love—These are emotions that stir the senses and produce love between a man and woman, which may lead to marriage. (Even in your fiftieth year of marriage, romantic love should continue to grow.)
- Brotherly love—This love shows concern for others in your community and around the world.

Love is a decision, a choice. Sometimes loving other people is hard and so you'll need the strength only God can give. Love is not always a set of flowery lines on a Hallmark greeting card. You must be the one to act when it comes to love. Make the apology, offer forgiveness, reach for a hand, give the hug, place the call, write the letter. Let love reign in your life, the way God intended it to reign, and be the one to initiate love whenever you have the chance.

Love is the doorway through which we pass from selfishness to service, from solitude to kinship with all mankind.

The Greatest of These

When Jesus taught he spoke about the heart. He stared down the high and mighty religious leaders and pulled their self-righteous stools right out from underneath them. No longer was it only wrong to kill, it was wrong to look at someone with hatred. The leaders clung to the commandment "Do not steal," but Jesus taught them about coveting—the consuming desire to own what someone else has.

A story in Mark tells about the greatest commandment of all. Jesus was hanging out with a group of Pharisees and Herodians—most of them trying to trip Jesus up, trying to get him to say something that would prove him to be a fraud. Of course, that never happened. Instead, Jesus taught them things they'd never heard before.

One of the teachers of the law came and heard them debating. He asked Jesus, "Of all the commandments, which is the most important?" (12:28, NIV).

"The most important one," answered Jesus, "is this: 'Hear, O Israel, the Lord our God, the Lord is one. Love the Lord your God with all your heart and with all your soul and with all your mind and with all your strength.' The second is this: 'Love your neighbor as yourself.' There is no commandment greater than these" (12:29–31, NIV).

What is the greatest thing you can do, the greatest thing you can invest in, the greatest way to live your life? Love God. Love others. That's a powerful lesson to remember your whole life.

High on Love

The former CEO of Southwest Airlines Herb Kelleher might just understand love better than any other person in his position. He once said, "We'd rather have a company run by love, not by fear. Perfect love drives out fear."

Want proof that love matters to the people at Southwest Airlines, and why the company is doing so well? Southwest flies out of Love Field in Dallas, the stock-exchange symbol Southwest uses is "LUV," the company newspaper is called *Luv Line,* and its twentieth anniversary slogan was, "Twenty Years of Loving You."

The employees at Southwest have stated, "Herb loves us. We love Herb. We love one another. We love the company."

In the midst of this love fest, many things have occurred:

- Southwest Airlines continues to do well, increasing its profits year after year.
- Employees at Southwest are more satisfied with their jobs than others in the same position.
- Passengers who fly Southwest are more likely to say they enjoyed the flight.

There's nothing like being high on love. Thirty thousand feet high!

Love Wins

Pastor John MacArthur recalls that when he came out of seminary, he was loaded up with truth, but short on patience.

"It was a strong temptation to come blasting into the church, dump the truth on everyone, and expect an immediate response," MacArthur says. "I needed to learn patience, tolerance, mercy, grace, forgiveness, tenderness, compassion—all the characteristics of love. It is wonderful to be bold and thunderous, but love is the necessary balance."

The lesson is true for us as well. A situation might not be fair. In fact, we might be right and the other person wrong. Truth might want to stand on a soapbox, whining and complaining about what's fair and right. But that's when love will win.

In the game of life, love always wins.

Play It Again, Schroeder . . .

In a well-loved *Peanuts* cartoon, Lucy asks Schroeder—who is playing the piano—if he knows what love is. Schroeder stands up, rigid and at attention, and begins to spout a definition he clearly knows by heart: "Love: A noun, referring to a deep, intense, ineffable feeling toward another person or persons."

Schroeder then sits down and returns to his piano. At that point, Lucy shakes her head and mutters, "On paper, he's great."

Understand everything you can about love, but then roll up your sleeves and live out the definition with all the people in your life. They need to see your love in action.

Satisfaction Guaranteed

Writer Richard Carlson once said, "I can almost guarantee you that someday, as you look back on your life, you'll be less interested in how many items and achievements you were able to collect than in how much you were able to express love."

Carlson is right. When you look at your future today, you may be inclined to dream about the things you'll accomplish, the ladders you'll climb, the goals you dream about attaining. All of those are good and are part of staying forever young. But love . . . ah, love is what will keep your heart and soul soft. Love is what will matter most at the end of your days.

When you're looking ahead, realize that one day you'll look back and smile wistfully at the life you're building. You'll look and you'll long for one more day with a special friend, one more conversation with your mother, one more hug from your dad, one more chance to dance with your true love.

You will definitely not look back and think about the promotion you did or didn't get, the awards you won for sales two decades earlier, or the bonus you received for work you won't even remember by then.

No, you'll look back and smile at the moments of love you shared. Don't leave anything undone. Love like there's no tomorrow and that way you'll have no regrets.

Even When It Hurts

You'll need to love in every situation, even when it hurts. Loving people is risky, because people are unpredictable sometimes. You may invest your heart in a person, only to have them walk out of your life or turn on you. When that happens you must ask yourself: "What have I lost for having loved?"

The answer is nothing. If you loved, you did the thing you were created and called to do. If you lost along the way, then go ahead and cry, but don't make the rash decision to never love again. You're the only one who is hurt by such a mind-set.

Writer Elizabeth Kübler-Ross once said, "To love means never to be afraid of the windstorms of life. Should you shield the canyons from the windstorms, you would never see the true beauty of their carvings."

And so it is with us. The windstorms will come, but love anyway. That's what Jesus wants us to do.

Love in a Nutshell

The Bible says that God is love. The following excerpt is from 1 John 4:7–21 (NIV). You will not find a better definition of love or a better guide about loving others:

Dear friends, let us love one another, for love comes from God. Everyone who loves has been born of God and knows God. Whoever does not love does not know God, because God is love. This is how God showed His love among us: He sent His one and only Son into the world that we might live through Him.

This is love: not that we loved God, but that He loved us and sent His Son as an atoning sacrifice for our sins. Dear friends, since God so loved us, we also ought to love one another. No one has ever seen God; but if we love one another, God lives in us and His love is made complete in us.

We know that we live in Him and He in us, because He has given us of His Spirit. And we have seen and testify that the Father has sent His Son to be the Savior of the world. If anyone acknowledges that Jesus is the Son of God, God lives in Him and He in God. And so we know and rely on the love God has for us.

God is love. Whoever lives in love lives in God, and God in him. In this way, love is made complete among us so that we will have confidence on the Day of Judgment, because in this world we are like Him. There is no fear in love. But perfect love drives out fear, because fear has to do with punishment. The one who fears is not made perfect in love.

We love because He first loved us. If anyone says, "I love God," yet hates his brother, he is a liar. For anyone who does not love his brother, whom he has seen, cannot love God, whom he has not seen. And He has given us this command: Whoever loves God, must also love his brother."

Follow the Leader

You will be called to lead in the years ahead. You will be fathers and mothers, leading children. Some of you will be managers or presidents of companies, some will be coaches, teachers or directors, captains or department chiefs. Someone reading this book might be president of the United States.

General Eric Shinseki, former army chief-of-staff, understood the connection between love and leadership. "You must love those you lead before you can be an effective leader," Shinseki said. "You can certainly command without that sense of commitment, but you cannot lead without it."

The best leaders are the ones who love those they are leading. Carolyn Peck, women's basketball coach of the University of Florida, once told me that the key to being a good coach is this: You've got to love your team.

Author Lance Secretan once said, "In my research into the greatest leaders in history, the ones we now revere most dearly, the ones that continue to inspire us most, the ones that we each know and love at a personal level today—they were the ones who had the greatest capacity to love."

So go . . . prepare in every way to take on the leadership position you are being called to, but remember to love. Only then will you be a leader worth following.

Spit It Out

Depending on the family you were raised in, love may be hard for you to articulate. Sure, you love your parents, your siblings, your friends. But for some of you, saying the words may be next to impossible.

Actions can say only so much, and no one can read your mind. One song that illustrates this is Reba McEntire's hit, "The Greatest Man I Never Knew," about a daughter reflecting on her deceased father. A line in the song says, "He never said he loved me, I guess he thought I knew."

Don't ever let that happen to you!

Those three little words—"I love you"—must not stay trapped in your heart, and die there, never spoken. If you've never said the words, next time you're with your mom or dad, look them in the eye and say these powerful words. "I LOVE YOU!"

Author Charles Swindoll has said, "'I love you.' Three simple, single-syllable words. Yet, they cannot be improved upon. Nothing even comes close. . . . We don't have any guarantee we'll have each other forever. It's a good idea to say those words as often as possible."

Start today. The people you love deserve to be told.

Twelve Words That Will Change Your Love Life

Sometimes we try too hard to make things right with the people we love.

If there's a conflict, remember the power of these twelve words:

- "I was wrong."   • "Please forgive me."
- "I am sorry."   • "I love you."

These words will keep the love flowing in every relationship you have, and help give you a life that is forever young.

Pat's Perspective

In 1967, the first Super Bowl game was played in Los Angeles. The Green Bay Packers of the NFL played the Kansas City Chiefs of the AFL. As the game approached, there was an enormous amount of excitement and eager anticipation to see who would win. After a tough battle, the Packers prevailed, but it was not easy.

After the game, the Packers' coach, Vince Lombardi, was interviewed on the field by a sideline reporter who asked him to reflect on his players. Lombardi replied that his players had great respect for each other, great admiration, deep loyalty, and then he paused for a minute and said, "What I'm trying to say is, they love each other."

I think that statement made the Lord happy because that's what he wants us to do. He wants us to love our families, our friends and our coworkers. He wants us to love the successful and the unsuccessful, the beautiful and the ugly, the upbeat and the downtrodden. He wants us to reach out with a heart full of love to everybody who crosses our path. Make that a high priority in your life starting today!

~

Love cures people. Both the ones who
give it and the ones who receive it.

—Dr. Karl Menninger, psychologist

We can judge others or we can love others.
We can't do both.

—Author unknown

Love can grow slowly, out of warmth
and companionship, and none of us
should be afraid to seek it.

—Ronald Reagan, former U.S. president

Only love can be divided endlessly,
and still not diminish.

—Anne Morrow Lindbergh, writer and aviation pioneer

If you have only one smile in you,
give it to the people you love. Don't be surly at home,
then go out in the street and start grinning,
"Good morning!" at perfect strangers.

—Maya Angelou, writer

Love has nothing to do with what you're
expecting to get. Rather it has only to do with
what you are expecting to give—
which is everything.

—Katharine Hepburn, actress

I still believe that love is all you need.
I don't know a better message
than that.

—Paul McCartney, singer and songwriter

Heart power is the strength of this world,
of America. And hate power is the
weakness of the world.

—Vince Lombardi, former NFL coach

Be wealthy in your friends.

—William Shakespeare, poet

The magic bullet of all healing is love.

—Dr. James W. Parker, author

A real friend is one who walks in, when
the rest of the world walks out.

—Walter Winchell, newspaper columnist

We cannot do great things on this Earth.
We can only do small things
with great love.

—Mother Teresa

Love is a game that two can play and both can win.

—Eva Gabor, actress

*If you're going to play together,
as a team, you've got to care for one another.
You've got to love each other.*

—Vince Lombardi, former NFL coach

*Racism is a sin of the heart.
We can force people to go to the same school
and eat at the same cafeteria, but we can't
force them to love one another.*

—J. C. Watts, Jr., former U.S. congressman

Acceptance is the activity of love.

—Samuel Kirshmer, writer

*Only those who love really live, in spite of
the pain it so often brings.*

—Eleanor Roosevelt, former first lady

*Kindness is the ability to love people
more than they deserve.*

—Author unknown

There are never enough "I love you's."

—Lenny Bruce, comedian

*What we once enjoyed and deeply loved,
we can never lose. For all that we love
deeply becomes a part of us.*

—Helen Keller, lecturer

*To love is to make one's heart
a swinging door.*

—Howard Thurman, theologian

*A joyful heart is the inevitable result of
a heart burning with love.*

—Mother Teresa

You can give without loving,
but you cannot love without giving.

—Amy Carmichael, missionary

One friend, one person who is truly
understanding, who takes the trouble to listen to
us as we express our problems, can change
our whole outlook on the world.

—Dr. Elton Mayo of Harvard University

The most powerful force in
all the earth is love.

—Nelson Rockefeller,
former governor of New York

Love is the most important word
in the English language.

—John Wooden,
former UCLA basketball coach

In Closing . . .

Now that you have a good handle on living life forever young, let's think back to the beginning of this book. It all started with God. He's the glue that holds every other piece of wisdom together.

Having a relationship with Christ is one of those principles that has to come first. Get that right, and everything else will seem easy. Pastor Matt Hannon of Washington State recently gave a series of sermons about everyday life. He based the series on the sorts of issues people talked to him about the most: relationships, money, sex, work and time.

Pastor Hannon's greatest advice in the series: Don't look around for wisdom when it comes to the important areas of life. Look up.

The people in life who learn the secret to holding on to their youth are those who have learned the secret of looking up. A great example is former president Ronald Reagan. During the time of Reagan's presidency, current North Carolina Senator Elizabeth Dole was a member of his White House staff and his cabinet.

"I was privileged to have a ringside seat for many of his most famous speeches," Dole said. "But the words of President Reagan that inspire me most were ones he shared with me when I served as Assistant to the President for Public Liaison."

Senator Dole sat alone with the president in a holding room before a speech he was set to give to a constituent group. Dole looked at him and said, "Mr. President, you have the weight of the world on your shoulders, yet you are always so kind and so gracious. How do you do it?"

President Reagan sat back and said, "Well, Elizabeth, when I was governor of California, each morning began with someone standing before my desk describing yet another disaster. The feeling of stress became almost unbearable. I had the urge to look over my shoulder for someone I could pass the problem to. One day, I realized that I was looking in the wrong direction. I looked up instead of back." He smiled at the senator, relaxed and at peace. "I'm still looking up. I couldn't face one more day in this office if I didn't know I could ask God's help and it would be given."

And so it is with you, graduate.

If you're to live your life forever young, you will need a relationship with the Creator of the Universe. You will need to walk with him and talk to him and ask for his help on every issue in your life. Then, as often as possible, you'll need to take President Reagan's advice.

Look up for the rest of your life!

About the Author

You can contact Pat Williams at:

Pat Williams
c/o Orlando Magic
8701 Maitland Summit Boulevard
Orlando, FL 32810
Phone (407) 916-2404
pwilliams@orlandomagic.com

Visit Pat William's Web site at:

www.patwilliamsmotivate.com

If you would like to set up a speaking engagement for Pat Williams, please write his assistant, Diana Basch, at the above address or call her at (407) 916-2454. Requests can be faxed to (407) 916-2986 or e-mailed to *dbasch@orlandomagic.com*.

We would love to hear from you. Please send your comments about this book to Pat Williams at the above address or in care of our publisher at the address below. Thank you.

Health Communications, Inc.
3201 SW 15th Street
Deerfield Beach, FL 33442